PURPOSE TO POWER

PURPOSE TO POWER

Your Journey to a Life of Meaning, Fulfillment, and Impact

DR. ANTHONY PERDUE

Purposeful Leaders Publishing

Copyright © 2021 by Dr. Anthony Perdue

All rights reserved. No part of this book may be reproduced in any manner whatsoever without written permission except in the case of brief quotations embodied in critical articles and reviews.

First Printing, 2021

I dedicate this book to my wife, Robin, whose encouragement and belief in me serve as a source of inspiration. To my children, AJ, Juliah, and Ava thank you for allowing me to show you a father's love. And to my mother, Rose, thank you for instilling purpose in me at a young age.

CONTENTS

ONE
PURPOSE AND WHY IT MATTERS TO YOU   1

  1 Purpose - The Search for True Life Meaning   2

  2 What Really is Purpose?   17

  3 The Power of Purpose   27

TWO
HOW TO FIND YOUR PURPOSE   **41**

  4 Finding Your Purpose Overview   42

  5 Purpose Through the Power of Your Story   46

  6 Purpose Through Self-Awareness   57

  7 Self-Awareness Through Values   69

  8 Self-Awareness Through Strengths   78

  9 Self-Awareness Through Emotional Intelligence   85

  10 Self-Awareness Summary   106

  11 Purpose Through Serving Others   110

  12 The Realization and Clarity of Purpose   119

THREE
HOW TO WALK IN YOUR PURPOSE — 129

   13 Purpose in Pictures – Creating Your Vision   130

   14 Execute!   147

   15 Purpose to Power: The Conclusion   159

Appendix   164

References   177

About The Author   186

PART ONE

Purpose and Why It Matters to You

CHAPTER 1

Purpose - The Search for True Life Meaning

"Live the Life of Your Dreams: Be brave enough to live the life of your dreams according to your vision and purpose instead of the expectations and opinions of others."
——Roy T. Bennett——

INTRODUCTION

In a small apartment in Landover, Maryland, a young seven-year-old boy once said, "mommy, where's my daddy?" A long pause ensued while the twenty-something single mother contemplated the question. As the young man stared at his mother, he couldn't help but notice the look of disgust and sadness in her eyes. He pursed his lips to the side as he concluded that his mother was ignoring the question.

"Well," he thought to himself, "my mom is ignoring me, and I have to eat fried chicken livers for dinner – again. What a terrible day?" The young boy slouched on the saggy couch in the dimly lit living room of the one-bedroom apartment. As the old TV started showing a zig-zag line, the boy stood to give it a whack in a failed attempt to adjust the screen. When that didn't work, the young boy took the pliers, placed them on the silver, half-moon-shaped metal nob, squeezed it, and changed the channel. When he found the cartoon that he was looking for, he adjusted the antennas with the aluminum foil on the ends. After a few minutes of his dealing with the TV, his mother finally spoke up, "I don't know where he is. Get ready for dinner."

As the strong scent of Crisco oil and fried chicken livers filled their air, the young boy wondered who he was. As he plopped back on the couch, he tried to put the thought of not having a dad out of his mind. He began to daydream of one day going to the moon. "Yes, I'll be an astronaut like Steve Austin," looking over at his six-million-dollar man action figure. The young boy didn't know who he was or why he was, but he dreamed. He dreamed of a circumstance beyond what he could realize about himself. He knew that he was going to do something big, something meaningful, something with purpose. His dream was interrupted by his mom, "Ant! Go wash your hands and come eat!"

As you may have already guessed, that young boy was me. Purpose for me has been personal, and I have been instilled with sense of it. Throughout my life, I have always felt like something was tugging on me. The gentle urging came from different directions and in various phases of life. As a young child, I always dreamed of a life bigger than the one I was experiencing. I would look up at the sky and ponder why I was born. The feeling I experienced as a seven or eight-year-old was one of understanding. I had the knowledge that I was born for a purpose, for a reason. You may recall having this experience at some point in your own life. Some of you may not have experienced this until you were older or may have never experienced it at all. If you are reading this, you most likely have asked the question, "why am I even here? What is my purpose for living?" You are not alone.

As I grew older and became a teenager, I felt that same tugging feeling, "Anthony, you are here for a purpose." When I started doing gymnastics at the late age of 14, I would often wonder if I was destined to be a great gymnast. By the time I was 17, I was an all-American gymnast, traveled the country competing, and had several colleges recruiting me. I even had the thought and the belief that I could go to the Olympics.

"I'm going to be the first black gymnast representing the United States," I would tell myself. Well, unfortunately that didn't happen. I did, however, earn a gymnastics scholarship to college, becoming the first one in my family ever to earn a college degree.

While I did go to college and performed as a collegiate gymnast, the tugging of purpose continued. Imagine a child standing next to his or her parent, yanking on their shirt while looking up with big brown eyes, asking, "what will I grow up to be?" My purpose has been like that child, tugging at me for years and years, wondering if I will ever grow up and become the adult I was meant to be. You see, to me, purpose is life. It is the very thing that makes life worth living and what most everyone desires - significance while on our planet known as earth.

THE IMPROBABLE JOURNEY OF YOU

I'd like you to pause a moment and take a deep breath. Go ahead, take a deep breath and exhale. When you do so, I'd like you to acknowledge that you just *are*. You *are* alive, you have breath in your lungs, and you can acknowledge your existence. Do you know that your probability of being alive and breathing fresh air is nearly zero? If left solely up to the probabilities of a dice role, you most certainly would not be reading this because you would not exist. But the great news is that you *are* alive, and now is your moment in time to *be* alive.

The improbability of us being alive is even greater when you consider the elements of time and space. Scientists place the age of the universe at about 13.7 billion years old. Earth is said to be about 4.54 billion years old. I don't know about you, but as Prince once said in the song Let's Go Crazy, "that's a mighty long time." If you can scale over four billion years, think about the fact that our lives are less than 100 years of this time. When I asked Google to calculate 100 / 4.54 billion, it came back with, "the answer is zero." In other words, our time on this planet is mathematically zero, or in layman's terms, nothing.

The concepts of space and distance in relation to our existence get even more astounding. The universe contains up to 200 sextillion stars (the equivalent of 21 zeros) known to scientists. Our sun is considered a star, which is one of 200 sextillions in existence. There are 200 billion galaxies in the universe, with the galaxy in which we live known as the Milky Way. Each galaxy has its own astounding number of suns (stars). The Milky Way alone has up to 400 billion stars.

If you think these numbers are breathtaking, think about it in terms of light speed and distance. The speed of light is 186,282 miles per second or about 670,616,629 mph. It takes approximately 1.3 seconds for light to travel to the moon and about 8 minutes to travel to the sun from the earth. I don't know about you, but I consider that to be amazingly fast! The universe is so large that even with all of this speed, it would take almost 14 billion years to reach what we currently know to be the end of the universe!

Our earth is the only known habitat of human life, and you are the result of an improbable journey! It gets even more amazing for you. Did you also know that you are *one* of 250 to 280 million sperm that traveled to reach the egg to become a fertilized life known as you! So yes, you are an improbable journey. So, given the fact that you are: a) part of a collection of 100 billion people to ever live on earth with the only known life, b) in a universe that is 13.7 billion years old and over 28 billion light-years in diameter, c) with over 200 sextillion suns (stars), and d) the winning sperm out of 250+ million sperms to reach the egg, to be fertilized and born!

Now for many of you, that was the easy part! Life itself has been a challenge, and yet you are still here. Many of us grew up in circumstances that some would simply not survive. Some of us have been homeless, motherless, fatherless, directionless, impoverished, malnourished, abused, used, traumatized, hypnotized, and victimized. Many of us have survived improbable situations where we should have been stabbed, shot, and died or just broken down to the point where we simply wanted to end our lives. In other words, "life ain't been no crystal stair." The poem, "Mother to Son," by Langston Hughes perhaps describes the challenges of life best in comparison to an old rickety stairwell:

Mother to Son, by Langston Hughes
Well, son, I'll tell you:
Life for me ain't been no crystal stair.
It's had tacks in it,
And splinters,
And boards torn up,
And places with no carpet on the floor-
Bare.
But all the time
I'se been a-climbin' on,
And reachin' landin's,
And turnin' corners,
And sometimes goin' in the dark
Where there ain't been no light.
So, boy, don't you turn back.
Don't you set down on the steps.
'Cause you finds it's kinder hard.
Don't you fall now-
For I'se still goin', honey,
I'se still climbin',
And life for me ain't been no crystal stair.

While the probability of what we consider "life on Earth" was so small, the probability of your life, your existence, and the ability for you to grow and thrive, and in some cases, even survive, may have been even smaller. For these reasons, you may be improbable, but you are purposeful. Ask yourself the following questions. What am I doing with my improbable journey? Am I living a life of purpose that reflects that magnificence of the improbable and the brevity of the time that I have been given on earth? Am I living a life of purpose that will make time and space irrelevant? Are my thoughts, decisions, and actions meaningful, purposeful, and powerful?

YOUR LIFE OF PURPOSE

Many of us continue to search for self-identity, significance, and self-worth in our existence. We may be adept at presenting a strong and confident outer shell, built on monuments of 'things' like our jobs, status, bank account, credit scores, marital status, clothes, looks, physique, degrees, or what we drive to name a few. Although those things can bring us, at times, short-term feelings of strength, they often leave us empty and unfulfilled in the long run.

Love, peace, joy, and a general sense of well-being are elusive characteristics that can only be sustained in true self-identity, worth, and understanding, along with purpose. When you know who you are and why you are, fulfillment comes in the pursuit of becoming your best self - to self-actualize.

Self-actualization is the final stage of human development coined by Abraham Maslow in his hierarchy of (human) needs. Self-actualization is when you truly become who you are meant to be and fully understand the highest version of yourself, your goals, and your acceptance of yourself in love and great worth. This realization of self gives you *your* true purpose and reflects the meaning of life to each of us individually. It is this realization that gives you true confidence in life. When you ask, what is the meaning of my life, purpose is what clarifies this question. Purpose is essential to life itself, and it is the driving force, not only to the significance of your life but to the power and fuel of fulfillment of life. It is *power*.

Your moment in time must have significance. That significance is your purpose. Your purpose is your reason for being - your very reason for life! What if someone walked up to you today and asked you, "what is your purpose for living?" What would you say, and how would you respond? That question is at the root of our significance as human beings. The question reveals what you believe your significance to be while here on earth. Purpose is the answer to significance, and significance gives us meaning and, therefore, fuel, focus, fulfillment, and ultimately *power*!

THE PURPOSELESS DRIVEN LIFE

The challenge is that many of us never get to experience what it truly means to live on purpose. Many live without purpose at all - *purposeless*. We can't see the forest for the trees because the daily grind of life and the challenges that are thrown our way can be all we can handle. I ask you not to accept that life and all of its challenges and problems be your leader. I ask that you be the leader of your life. You are the master of your fate and the captain of your soul.

There are many impediments to leading and living your life to the fullest. I believe that the largest impediments to living a life on purpose are that we a) don't know who we really are, truly understanding our own self-identity, b) have bound and adapted to an existing popular culture driven by corporate greed and money, and c) are bound to a painful and traumatic history, whether familial, cultural, or other. These impediments have forced us to accept and identify ourselves in popular culture norms, where we are stuck in an identity outside of who we really are, never finding and living out our true purpose in life.

In his book, *The Fifth Mountain*, Brazilian novelist Paulo Coelho writes a fictionalized version of the Prophet Elijah's story, who struggles throughout his life to fulfill his purpose as a prophet. Elijah experienced powerful visions as a child and young man and was told by a priest that he was a "man of the spirit," able to hear God. In other words, he was destined to be a prophet. Elijah's parents, however, connected more to the ideal of what was a popular secular vocation of the time. His parents rejected his designation as a prophet and made him train for the vocation as a carpenter instead.

After many trials, doubts, and tribulations, Elijah eventually self-realizes, finds significance, and ultimately accepts his purpose. Unfortunately, he lost out on many, many years of potential influence and the experience of walking in his purpose. Think about what could have been had he not rejected who he actually was.

WHO AM I?

The question before you now is, do you know who you are? If someone walked up to you right now and asked the question, "hi there, who are you?" What would be your answer? How would you respond? Would you identify yourself with just your name? Would you identify yourself as what you do in your job - your title or work? One of the most frequent responses to this question, besides your name, is around what you *do*. For example, if you are a computer programmer or cyber security expert, you may respond, "I am a computer expert who helps companies discover security breaches."

Are you really any of those things? Are you really your job, your title, or even a member of a family lineage? I bet if you take a moment to think about it, you probably don't think that you *are* any of those things. You might even say to yourself, "well, I guess those things may be a part of who I am, but not really *who* I am." Are you losing out on years of your life like Elijah, not understanding who you really are, and living in your purpose?

The very first challenge of living with purpose is understanding who we really are. Many of us don't even know who we are, which feeds confusion, distraction, anxiety, worry, self-medication, and being led astray. This problem contributes to a lack of clarity of how we fit into the world. Worse yet, we fit into the world in ways we are not supposed to.

Why is it that many of us are without purpose and live directionless or misdirected lives? To quote a line from the movie *Malcolm X* by Spike Lee, I assert that "You've been had! Ya been took! Ya been hoodwinked! Bamboozled! Led astray! Run amok!" Yes, I believe that cultural and historical factors have contributed to our current state of aimlessness and purposelessness. The antidote to being led astray is self-identity - being able to know who you truly are.

According to research, self-identity refers to the need to understand a clear sense of self. Self-identity consists of self-knowing, self-expression, and maintaining self over time (attachment to the past and ancestry). These three self-identity elements are inextricably linked, suggesting that all three make up what is known as psychological ownership. This trio of self-identity elements helps drive your ability to feel as though you are tied to something, like an object, target, or a safe place. In other words, "there's no place like home."

The term "know thyself" has been used in multiple contexts throughout history. Knowing who we are can mean many different things to different people. Ultimately it is up to each individual to define him or herself. We can define ourselves in a number of ways. The totality of our thoughts and feelings towards ourselves concerning our abilities, limitations, appearance, values, characteristics, and personality are some of the ways we define ourselves.

CONFORMING TO THIS WORLD (CULTURAL IDENTITY)

The second biggest challenge to living with purpose is fighting against popular culture, which is imposed on us each and every second of the day. The pull of cultural adaptation is likened to a roaring lion pacing back and forth, licking its chops, waiting on your every move. This lion is not a normal lion. This lion is cunning and can act as if he is your friend. This lion can chew you up and spit you out while you think you're the one chomping on a tasty meal. This lion can force you to adapt to its ways and become what it wants you to become without you even knowing it.

For most of the history of human existence, tribes, families, and communities have been built around and upon culture. Culture is the foundation of the knowledge, understanding, meanings, and values that infuse all aspects of our lives, from how we think and act, to how we see ourselves in the world. The culture in which we live becomes a source of our self-understanding and self-identity.

Culture can be extraordinarily strong in its connection to who we are. Traditions passed down from generation to generation shape how we express ourselves in enjoying art, music, and dance to storytelling, literature, and stage performances. Culture gives us the norms of our values, principles, and ethics, our sense of wrong and right. The language we speak, the clothes we wear, and how we style our hair are all driven by culture. Culture is powerful. In cultures built upon our highest values of love, connectedness, and serving one another, this can be a positive and powerful contribution to our self-concept.

But what happens when culture is built on values of fear, every man and woman for themselves, or individualism? What happens when everything that you think, feel and act on has been programmed in you, convincing you that more is always better. This type of culture can have a devastating effect on who you are.

Our current (western) culture is based heavily on the almighty dollar and corporations' ability to drive increased profits, stock price growth, and shareholder value. These norms often take precedence over morality, ethics, and values. There is a literal fight for your soul and self-identity, waged by corporations (that many of us work for, by the way) that care (mostly) about money. Cultural norms are defined by the rich and powerful and can control how we think, feel and act on a daily basis.

Stop and think for a minute about what you did today. If you wrote down everywhere you went, every action you took, and every desire in your heart, many of your thoughts or actions were most likely derived from a marketing campaign or cultural norm influence campaign began by a corporation. I'm not here to bash companies or tell you to go live in a cave or igloo, but I think we all need to be aware of a main source and root of how we often define ourselves.

Does this sound a bit farfetched? Well, let me give you some food for thought. Literally, billions of dollars are spent on marketing, vying for your attention, action, and money. In fact, social media companies use the same techniques as the gambling industry to activate the same brain mechanisms triggered by cocaine to get you to engage on their platforms to maximize their profits! For many of us, the first action of the day is to check our social media accounts to get that morning high. I wish this were an exaggeration. The former Vice President of User Growth of Facebook told an audience of Stanford students that "the short-term, dopamine-driven feedback loops that we have created are destroying how society works." In other words, we have all been treated like crackheads - given drugs in exchange for money driven by advertising dollars.

Our thoughts and perceptions about our lives are shaped by what we see and hear on YouTube, Facebook, Instagram, Snapchat, TikTok, and other such platforms. At times, we have no choice but to be down with OPP - a life too often defined by *other people's problems* or *other people's promises*. Both our mental and emotional states are deeply affected. Have you ever seen an IG or Facebook post that caused you to *feel* bad? Perhaps someone you know presented a picture of himself popping' bottles in the club or on the beach? How about those beautiful pictures of the perfect family? Sadly, the overwhelming majority of what is presented to us is either a) fake, b) grossly exaggerated, c) half of the story, or d) considerably immoral or unethical. The challenge with this is that as you spend time on these mediums, these images, videos, and posts, shape who you are. You think what you see and hear and *literally* are what you think. As a man thinketh, so shall he be!

I'm not here to bash all social media, but I'm here to make you *aware* that it can be a huge source of feelings of fear, worry, anxiety, uncertainty, doubt, and guilt, shaping how you think, feel and ultimately act. Your identity and who you are, have been, and are being shaped by monetary pursuits. You *are* being eaten by the lion whose main objective is to make money.

THE HISTORICAL CONTEXT OF CULTURE

The third and potentially most devastating impediment to living a life of purpose is cultural history. You and I are bound to our cultural history, whether we like it or not. This history can be defined by our family and ancestors and can have traumatic effects on how we see ourselves. A cultural history with constant reinforcement of power, prestige, and prominence will yield the same individualized feelings. It may be easier for us to adopt and adapt to a self-identity that reflects said power, prestige, and prominence.

In contrast, a culture that has been built out of pain, worthlessness, and powerlessness will yield those same feelings in the individuals that are a part of that culture. In fact, as many of us seek to better ourselves, our lives, and the lives of our families, we are engaged in a constant tug-of-war, a duality of the mind, between the traumatic, negative circumstances of culture, and the positive present and future we faithfully set for ourselves.

For example, I am an African American, and I assert that our culture has been severely harmed, first and foremost, from the abominable truth of the slave trade from Africa to America. According to the Trans-Atlantic Slave Trade Database, over 12.5 million Africans were shipped to the New World from Africa, with 10.7 million surviving. It is estimated that about 450,000 Africans were brought to North America between 1525 and 1866, which is said to be the entirety of the history of the slave trade. If you are wondering about the math, the overwhelming majority were shipped to the Caribbean and South America. Today, 42 million African Americans live in the United States, who directly descended from this original group of 450,000. I find this personally astounding.

Astounded or not, the reality is that 42 million of us are descendants of a systematic deculturization where, not only were we stripped of culture, but it was replaced with trauma-filled, dehumanizing attributes based upon extreme fear, violence, and oppression. This dehumanizing of African Americans has unfortunately lingered up and through the 21st century, where black and brown children are shot, killed, and kidnapped disproportionately, while a desensitized population, lacking empathy and social responsibility, turn the other cheek and fight back when attention is drawn to these injustices.

Yes, the devastating effects of slavery still exist today. According to a study that evaluated the racial disparities in health and wealth due to slavery and discrimination, African Americans are much less likely to experience positive life changes, including those for a life of good health and wealth. A recent study concluded that African American students, grades 8 - 10, proactively protected themselves from failure by detaching their self-esteem from their academic outcomes. In other words, these students began to disassociate themselves from their schoolwork to protect their self-worth. African Americans were beaten for learning to read, killed for possessing books, and lynched for speaking in an educated manner to their white counterparts. This protection through academic dissociation is a mechanism for protection from a cultural history of trauma and pain.

This cultural history phenomenon also explains why some African Americans associate themselves more strongly with being "light-skinned" or "acting white." Most African Americans are not under a spell, thinking that they are passing for white (although some have bleached their skin in hopes of getting closer). Studies show that some African Americans frequently give themselves a mixed-race identity to get closer to an advantaged group (e.g., white American) while distancing themselves from their own perceived disadvantaged group. This same study found that by "rejecting blackness and acting white," many African Americans have better education, better jobs, and greater wealth. This perhaps explains why many of us, both currently and in recent history, straighten our hair, wear blue-eyed contact lenses, and align ourselves and our self-identity more with that of the mainstream or white America than we do black America.

Cultural history can significantly affect how we see ourselves, our self-identity, and ultimately our purpose. Our true sense of self and purpose can be profoundly inhibited without overcoming latent and blatant current, and historical factors - with all of the beatings, rape, forced labor, separation of families, and the list goes on and on. Many African Americans have still managed to understand and find their self-identity, self-love, and self-esteem. They have walked in their purpose and have become juggernauts in their life's work. So, there is hope for each and every one of us regardless of our race or skin color. However, in many cases, we have to understand the roots of the problems of purpose to live *in* purpose.

THE IDENTITY GAP

For many of us, a gap exists, or once existed, between self-identity and what can be known as cultural norms. This can create a juxtaposed sense of self, reflected in two distinct but related selves known as the actual self and the ideal self. The actual self is how a person sees him or herself in the here and now. The actual self is our true self-identity, where our purpose can lay dormant, that we can choose to embrace, building upon our authenticity driven by our gifts, values, principles, and personality.

On the other hand, we have the ideal self, which is how a person would like to see him or herself, especially in relation to the culture. This is often an ideal of self-identity and purpose, not of our own, but a cultural pretext driven by popular culture, money, and in many cases, a history of trauma, violence, and devastation.

Some of us have rejected that our ideal self has to be a reflection of the culture. In fact, some have chosen an ideal self based on their religion or belief system or another counter-cultural representation such as self-empowerment, family culture, or black empowerment. For others, it is a game of survival. We "survive in the gap" between our actual self and the cultural ideal. There are typically three ways of this survival: 1) adaption, 2) medication, or 3) undulation.

When we adapt, we accept the ideal and form our self-identity around the culture. We have adapted to know the ideal and the thinking, feeling, and acting of cultural norms. In this instance, our speech, dress, activities, and habits strongly reflect the culture. For others, we self-medicate to deal with the gap. We indulge in substances such as food, alcohol, porn, drugs, excessive video game play, as well as other mind and emotion-numbing activities. Lastly, we undulate rising and falling to whatever occasion in which we are involved. This is sometimes called code switching or acting differently in different environments.

IT'S TIME TO LIVE ON PURPOSE

The time is now to live who you are and take back your true reason for being. The time is now for you to know, understand, and live your true identity and purpose. There is a fierce urgency for you to find your purpose and walk in it each and every day, leaving your mark in this blip in time and space.

You were born for a reason. I imagine that you are reading this book right now because you know, either deep down or very overtly, that your life has purpose and meaning - that you were born for a reason. More importantly, you may be looking for a true identity and believe that purpose will help give you a better understanding of and a direction for your life. I believe that knowing who you are and why you were born definitely will.

It is time to throw off the cape of fear, worry, and anxiety and get out of the gap between your true self and the culture's ideal. It's time to focus on who you were meant to be and have the freedom of choice regardless of a preconceived level of popularity in the culture. Don't be eaten by the lion. Feed the lion and influence it to be shaped in the image of your truth, your identity, and your purpose. Clarify your purpose and direction for your life to achieve a sense of self-worth, identity, greatness, and well-being, all of which is POWER!

CHAPTER 2

What Really is Purpose?

"Definiteness of purpose is the starting point of all achievement."
———*W. Clement Stone*———

A PURPOSEFUL MOMENT

On Saturday, May 6th, the year 2017, I heard them call my name. "Doctor Anthony Perdue," someone said, and I could hear the echo and reverberation of the sound of my name in the auditorium. As I began to take steps toward the Dean of the School of Business, time seemed to slow to a crawl. The reverbing sound of my name, the cheers and applause from the crowd, and the enthusiastic sounds of pride and happiness of my mother and my then-fiancé were muffled in my mind but joyfully present. I had finally accomplished a major milestone in my purpose and mission. I had completed my Doctor of Strategic Leadership.

As I continued my walk across the well-lit stage, I reflected on my discovery of purpose about seven years earlier. I remember reading the book *Life on Purpose* by Dr. Brad Swift. His book sparked within me a true understanding of what I was sent to earth to accomplish. I discovered that my purpose was to help others find their purpose and be the best leaders they could be for themselves, their families, their businesses, their communities, and all of the domains in which they have leadership. I realized that my gift was understanding the nature of spiritual, social, and scientific aspects of life and that it was my God-given purpose and path to help others become purposeful leaders.

That reflection also brought about thoughts of the improbable journey. During the past seven years, I had personally experienced such life-changing loss that it would seem that the probability of my earning a Doctoral degree was nearly impossible. I had gone through a rough divorce and had been laid off from a job of 18 years at IBM. There were times when I literally felt like I wouldn't make it to the next day.

As I reached for my degree, I was overcome with joy. The joy of an accomplishment in the journey of my purpose was overwhelming. I knew that I had reached a major milestone, but I also knew that I was just *beginning* to live my life on purpose and that the work would not be easy, but the journey would be full of meaning and sustainable joy - of power! I knew that my blip in space and time, in a universe in which its size boggles the imagination, had meaning and that I would have a purposeful impact on the planet.

That impact is to be realized by helping you to find your purpose and helping you to be the best purposeful leader that you can be, utilizing all of your God-given gifts and talents so that *you* may have a meaningful impact on the planet. My purpose is to be your guide and assist you through your journey. Your challenge will be to filter through all of the noise of the culture, of a painful past, and to become the ultimate author, director, and producer of your own story. You are the lead role in your life's story, the ultimate hero who will clarify and embark on the journey of your life's purpose.

UNDERSTANDING PURPOSE

Purpose has had its ups and downs in popularity as a concept. The most basic definition of purpose, according to dictionary.com, is "the reason for which something exists or is done, made, used, etc." The application of purpose, however, is far from a basic concept in our lives.

Purpose in the context of human existence includes the basic definition of reason. However, understanding purpose from spiritual, psychological, and philosophical contexts should be explored for the full understanding and relevance of purpose in our lives. This full understanding will ground the rest of this book as you explore your own purpose and the key principles and framework to walk in your purpose.

SPIRITUAL PURPOSE

The most notable text and movement in the realm of spiritual purpose came with the release of Rick Warren's, *The Purpose Driven Life*. The New York Times bestseller, released in 2002, has sold more than 32 million copies and has been published in 85 languages. Warren proved that purpose in spiritual and Godly manifestation was and continues to be a relevant part of popular culture.

The Greek word for purpose is boúlomai, which means a resolute plan that "underlines the predetermined (and determined) intention driving the planning" from God, always working out for His (God's) purpose. In other words, God ordains our predetermined or predestined plans intentionally, in conjunction with human existence on earth. According to Biblical teachings, although we have free will, God has a preordained purpose (or plan) for our lives.

Spiritual purpose has roots in the concept of work. Dr. Martin Luther King, Jr. lived out his purpose in his work which, in large part, defined the civil rights movement. His last speech, delivered on April 3, 1968, outlined his life's work and purpose. His purpose cost him his life, but he viewed his work as God's will:

> *"But it doesn't matter with me now. Because I've been to the mountaintop. And I don't mind. Like anybody, I would like to live a long life. Longevity has its place. But I'm not concerned about that now. I just want to do God's will. And He's allowed me to go up to the mountain. And I've looked over. And I've seen the promised land. I may not get there with you. But I want you to know tonight that we, as a people, will get to the promised land. And I'm happy tonight. I'm not worried about anything. I'm not fearing any man. Mine eyes have seen the glory of the coming of the Lord."*

The Bible similarly describes Jesus. John 9:4 says, "I must work the works of Him who sent Me while it is day; the night is coming when no one can work." Jesus believed that there was limited time on earth to do what God has called us to do and that we should have an urgency about our purpose (our work) because of that limited time. Ben Witherington, III describes the God of the Bible as the pre-eminent worker, and He expects the same of His followers. In other words, your purpose is your life's work, according to the Biblical perspective.

Purpose also extends beyond work and our *doing* to who we are and our *being*. Our being is rooted in the inward and outward expression of our values, also known as character. Indian scriptures assert that specific values such as love are the essence of the divine and express themselves as spiritual values such as peace, truth, love, freedom, harmony, self-giving, and unity. The more one lives by these values, the higher spiritual consciousness (holy Samskaras) one will achieve, thereby perceiving more truth and reality in one's life that reflects our highest purpose.

PSYCHOLOGICAL PURPOSE

The psychological approach to purpose takes the form of the intentionality of the mind. The assertion that you are the master of your fate and create your own life purpose or purposes *is* to have purpose. The ability to have purpose stems from an effort to recognize your purpose through challenging the very values we hold dear. Values reflect what is important to us in life, in a psychological sense, and can be expressed as a preferred end-state (terminal value) or a mode of conduct (instrumental value). Either of these values can be categorized as follows: 1) defensive values, helping us to defend ourselves against threats, real or perceived; 2) stabilizing values, adjusting to, and maintaining the status quo; and 3) growth values, progressing forward to the achievement of our potential across various areas including creativity, innovation, knowledge, flexibility, trust, and integrity.

Values and the way we see ourselves can be the difference between a full tank of gas, fuel for our purpose, or driving on empty, led by defensive values or a place of lack. In their book, *The Power of Full Engagement*, Jim Loehr and Tony Schwartz see values as core to defining purpose. Values such as integrity, respect for others, gratitude, excellence, service, and self-care, drive our purpose and become a significant energy source, especially when they move from negative to positive in our lives.

People who see life as threatening, cold, and lacking, and perhaps feel cheated, may find it difficult to find spiritual or intrinsic meaning in life itself. In other words, the ability for someone to find purpose and meaning in life is a reflection of how they see life itself from a deep sense of self-worth and values.

This sense of self and our values also align with our well-being. In one study, the authors posited that "four key experiences were found to promote meaning and purpose in life: 1) physical and mental well-being, 2) belonging and recognition, 3) personally treasured activities and 4) spiritual closeness and connectedness." The more we feel good physically and are connected to others and spiritual power, the more likely we are to find and promote our own purpose.

PHILOSOPHICAL PURPOSE

There are several schools of philosophical perspectives on the meaning of life and purpose. As you can imagine, whole books can and have been written on the philosophy of life's meaning. The perspectives range widely and vary based on the culture and time frames of human history.

For example, in Africa, Mr. Fred Swaniker, a Ghana-born social entrepreneur, believes that we are defined by our moments of obligation. During his interview to become recognized as one of the world's youngest and best social entrepreneurs, he was asked about his moment of obligation. For Fred, being asked that question revealed to him his purpose. He realized that his 'moments of obligation' crystalized his ability to become focused on his main purpose, born out of a sense of outrage and acknowledging the injustice and wrongdoing in African leaders. Fred found his obligation through what he wanted to see changed for his fellow countrymen and women's good and betterment.

As a result, he formed the African Leadership Academy and was determined to ignore the other 99% of his 'moments of obligation.' Fred recognized his purpose, his main obligation, and has been determined to focus on his main purpose while ignoring everything else. While I cannot say that Fred's reflective moment and dedication represent an African philosophy on purpose, I can say that Fred's realization of 'moments of obligation' reflects a philosophical approach to purpose and meaning in life that can be admired.

Another approach to purpose that has been studied is that of Greek philosophy, which forms the basis of the western view of purpose. Although several Western philosophies are related to purpose, the study and focus on living a life of virtue have dominated popular discourse. Plato is widely considered to be the father of western philosophy and offered an early perspective on life's meaning and purpose. Plato espoused the idea that life's meaning was understood by attaining the highest form of knowledge that leads to being and doing good. Being and doing good is based upon the knowledge and application of the four cardinal virtues of human excellence: *wisdom, temperance, courage, and justice.*

Aristotle builds upon Plato's argument and purports that man's ultimate goal, and purpose is to attain good. He believed that eudaimonia, the expression of happiness in humans functioning at our absolute best through our highest virtues, was the key to living out our ultimate purpose. This philosophical approach provides a strong correlation with both the spiritual and psychological explorations of purpose as it deals with a focus on virtues, which aligns with both psychological values and the attainment and life application of spiritual principles that reflect a Godly mandate of the highest calling for mankind. To put it simply, spiritual, psychological, and philosophical views point to acquiring knowledge of virtues, growth values, and Godly principles and their application in who we are and what we do that expresses the highest form of good in our lives.

THE CHALLENGE OF PURPOSE

As you very well know by now, I am most passionate in my belief that everyone has a purpose, a mission in life, a reason for being. However, so very few people have an understanding of their purpose in life.

We all have a calling, a reason for being, a purpose, a mission. The challenges that most people face today are that they a) do not realize that they have a purpose, b) do not find it useful or relevant to their lives, c) realize that purpose is a reality but do not know their purpose, and d) are unable to nurture their purpose into an expression of who they are and what they do in their lives.

It has been said that less than 10% of people have goals. I would venture to guess that an even smaller percentage would be able to express their purpose. I believe that goals and even a vision are things people generally understand, especially related to purpose as it pertains to their lives. Most of us think about obtaining some *thing* or some object like losing weight or making more money. These are goals. Having purpose is much more esoteric and often hard to grasp in reality to ones' existence. Taking the question of "what is your purpose" further, some might respond, "the heck if I know!" Purpose is often a distant thought in the lives of people who may be just trying to get to the next day, put food on the table, and gas in the car.

The second challenge of purpose is that some people do not find it relevant to their lives. They might say, "having a purpose really doesn't matter." How is having a purpose both relevant and helpful to me? The short answer is that purpose helps us with the one thing that drives us forward - growth. Having a growth mindset gives us hope for moving forward, up and outward! The other significance of purpose in our lives is that it helps us define who we are. Most people look for their significance in either what they do (i.e., their job title), what they have (e.g., cars, houses, clothes), or through their personification or who they portray themselves to be to the world through outward appearances and social media. I am not here to discourage anyone from finding significance in those things, but I am here to reveal to you that having purpose brings a greater significance that job titles, possessions, and our social media status cannot give. Our purpose and those things can go hand in hand. For example, your purpose can fuel your social media presence, brand, and content. Your purpose can influence your personal style. And as you will find, as you read on, purpose can influence your work, goals, plans, and even your day-to-day actions.

The next challenge, and perhaps the most discomforting, is that while they find purpose relevant, most people simply don't know their purpose. You might honestly believe that understanding your reason for being is significant, but you just have no clue what it is. I think this is where most people find themselves. A study showed that nearly 90% of people considered themselves spiritual, believing in a higher power. This belief drives a knowledge that they have been a) created by this higher power, b) created with a purpose, and c) blessed with certain gifts, talents, and life circumstances to use to fulfill this purpose.

Think of not knowing your purpose like this. Imagine getting on a boat. The boat is fairly nice and has a row of seats inside with no windows. The boat starts moving, but you have no idea where it's going. All you see are television screens inside the boat in place of windows that bombard you with advertisements, bright lights, and loud sounds.

Meanwhile, you notice someone who looks like he works on the boat, and you ask where the boat is going. He replies, "we have no destination." This is how living life without purpose feels. We board a boat called life, we get inundated with distractions, and forget that we were supposed to be going somewhere and that there is a journey that is supposed to look much, much different. Your journey is your purpose. Your purpose has both destiny and direction.

The good news is that knowledge of your purpose may be closer than you think. You may already be walking in it but do not fully recognize it because of all of the noise coming at you from social media, television, and other distractions. We are living in a time where choices and the fight for our attention is at an all-time high. Literally, billions of dollars are spent to try to get your attention and send you down a rat hole, or at least in a direction that you previously did not plan. Clarity of purpose can help you sift through all of the noise.

The last challenge of purpose is knowing how to nurture it to adulthood - to your power! One of the most fulfilling feelings in life is to know why we are born and work, play, and live in that realization often, always, and all days. Purpose gives us a sense of achievement, whether you are an athlete that spends her waking moments preparing for competition and working out or a father who has dedicated his time to staying at home to raise his children. The challenge comes when we feel stuck in doing a job or being in a situation where we realize that it is not aligned with our purpose. *Purpose to Power* is about shifting who we are and what we do in expression of our purpose. True power is in living and walking in your purpose as an expression of your highest values and virtues, as well as in the work of your hands, heart, and mind.

PURPOSE SUMMARY

It has been said that finding your purpose in life is like finding treasure. The size of this treasure or the realization of your potential and purpose can be found in your expression of values. Pablo Picasso has a quote that I think sums up purpose as an outward expression of our inward selves. His quote states, "The meaning of life is to find your gift, the purpose of life is to give it away." My hope is that you find your purpose and experience the wonderful urgency of walking in it, meeting your 'moment of obligation.'

Ultimately, our purpose is linked to who we are, our values, and our sense of well-being. There is a common thread across psychology, Christianity, and Indian and Socratic literature. An adaptation of growth values to your life determines the highest realization of the meaning of life. If you can think of your own values and personality on a dartboard, purpose would be at the innermost, concentric circle. Your identity and how you see yourself shapes your understanding and belief in your ultimate purpose. Purpose is defined by the intent or reason for our lives. Whether you believe it is God-given or an essential element of your mental intentionality or values, you have a purpose.

Purpose is characterized by the very definition and meaning of the journey of our lives. Although we may never attain an end state in our purpose, you are the main character in your lifelong story and are the author of that purpose and journey. The question is, are you willing to take up the call to discover your reason for being and go forth and conquer in your purpose? We will explore further the power of purpose, purpose discovery, and an approach for you to walk in your journey of purpose.

CHAPTER 3

The Power of Purpose

"The successful person has the habit of doing things failures don't like to do. They don't like doing them either necessarily. But their disliking is subordinated to the strength of their purpose."
——*Stephen Covey*——

I'd like you to take a moment to reflect on the word *power*. Before reading this chapter, I'd like you to take a couple of minutes to write the first thoughts that come to mind when you think of the word *power*. What's your personal definition of power? What keywords, characteristics, or attributes come to mind? What pictures or visions do you see when you contemplate the word? Be as specific as possible about what power looks like for you. Ask yourself the question, "what would I be and do if I were powerful?" How would you feel being powerful? Think about all of your life areas where being powerful would be not only appropriate but desired. Describe what it looks like in the different areas of your life. What would it look like to live with great power *within* you?

When I think of the power of me, I think of:

_____

_____

_____

What exactly is "power" when it comes to a person? We often think of power in the context of leadership, where a politician, CEO, or someone in a prominent position or stature may have power. While it is true, in one sense, that a person can have power from a position of authority or high office, it is also true that a person can have power in who she is - in their *being*. We have been sold through history and movies that the person who holds the power has the power. They have the distinct feeling of ultimate control, where the winds can change around them at the snap of a finger.

I assert that the power each of us has lay *within* us. In your answer above, you may have described how power can manifest itself in several ways, including spiritually, financially, emotionally (e.g., confident or courageous), mentally, and physically.

The Oxford dictionary defines power beginning with four related but distinct areas:

1. The **ability** to do something or act in a particular way, especially as a faculty or quality;
2. The **capacity** or ability to direct or influence the behavior of others or the course of events;
3. Physical **strength** and **force** exerted by something or someone;
4. **Energy** is produced by mechanical, electrical, or other means and used to operate a device.

This definition focused on human behavior makes it even more interesting. Personal power is your ability, your capacity, your strength, and your energy to act, produce, direct, or influence someone or something. When you have a clear and thoughtful purpose, you have this power. In fact, you have the maximum positive energy exerted in an effort to move life forward in the most effective and efficient way possible. In other words, it is the maximum amount of 'realized' purposeful energy towards a positive outcome, or set of outcomes, in the most efficient manner possible. You can be, you can do, and you can achieve anything with your purposeful energy and power!

When I was growing up, a song was often sung in the church by the elders. The church ladies would sing, "this little light of mine, I'm gonna let it shine, let it shine, let it shine, let it shine." This song had it right! Your power is your light. Your light is everything you are! Let me say that again. Your light (your power) is EVERYTHING that YOU are! It is bringing your best self to the party of life and burning up the dance floor! The question is, what is your light and how bright is it?

The power of purpose cannot and should not be underestimated. A purpose can literally move a mountain, create a city or country, or determine life and death. Purpose can be a beautiful obsession towards a changing circumstance beyond the imagination. Purpose can uplift those in times of sorrow and despair; even in the darkest moments of our lives, it can provide hope from hopelessness and light out of the depths of darkness. It is both an energizing force towards powerful life outcomes and a recipient of life's energy back towards its own growth. Purpose is like the sun, a seemingly infinite source of energy. The outcomes of purpose feed back into itself, making it an even more powerful element.

Purpose is one of the greatest sources of human energy. Purpose is power! There are countless reasons why living with purpose is advantageous to your life. We all have a purpose that has been born to us. Let's take a deeper look at the power of purpose in the various areas of our lives.

PURPOSE FOR BETTER OVERALL HEALTH & WELLBEING

I want you to live to 100 years old in the healthiest, happiest way possible! "May you live 100 years" is a term used throughout certain cultures to wish you a long life of well-being, happiness, and purpose. The challenge for many of us is finding or knowing someone who is 100 years old, "alive and kicking," is a rarity, to say the least. The good news is that people can and do live to 100 years old and beyond. These people are known as centenarians. How do they do it? They find a life purpose, among other things.

In the Caribbean hotspot known as Nicoya, Costa Rica, a central theme of their residents is "plan de vida," which translates as "a reason to live." This plan de vida is a main ingredient to their secret to longevity. Their sense of purpose "...often results in centenarians retaining an active lifestyle, reaping the benefits of physical activity and exposure to the sun." In fact, a 60-year-old Costa-Rican man has roughly twice the chance of living to 90 as a man living in the United States. They are extremely family-oriented, providing support for one another and living with purpose to positively affect the greater good.

What these Costa Ricans have is a keen sense of well-being. Well-being refers to how people experience and evaluate their lives, often through the lens of their emotional and cognitive evaluative responses, satisfaction, and states of being. According to Michaelson, Mahony, and Schifferes (2012), well-being emphasizes how people feel and function on personal and social levels and evaluate their lives overall. Generally, well-being is related to how we feel (e.g., happiness and life satisfaction) and how we function (e.g., self-realization, purpose, and relationships with others). Ask yourself, "how do I feel right now?" You might feel happy, sad, mad, glad, anxious, worried, or something else. How you feel in the moment is what is referred to as subjective feelings. It is also related to the hedonic school of thought, or what is known as hedonism. On the other hand, positive psychological functioning is what we think of when we examine our potential as human beings. Known as the eudemonic approach, this includes concepts such as finding meaning and purpose, positive relationships, self-determination, and autonomy.

There have been debates on the merits of measurement of well-being between the hedonic and eudemonic approaches dating back to ancient Greece. Think of it this way. You can find happiness and joy in a bottle of Grey Goose or a hit of marijuana, but that doesn't necessarily mean that you live a life of well-being. Brain depressants and stimulants can make us feel "happy" at the moment, but can be used or abused to mask a life of depression, sadness, pain, or even trauma. On the other hand, positive psychological functioning means that our lives are fulfilling over the long run and reflect a true state of happiness and well-being. This is what the Costa Rican centenarians experience. They experience a lifetime of well-being, driven in large part by a strong sense of purpose.

Although living to 100 is a nice goal for all humans, many of us would just appreciate living a purposeful, stress-free life of well-being in the now, full of life and free of health challenges. Well, there's good news for you too. A recent study from the Harvard Medical School concluded that having a life purpose can help keep you healthy through three main pathways. First, purpose makes you more likely to protect your health. You are more likely to eat better, sleep better, and increase your focus on preventative health services. Second, purpose may help reduce stress because you are less bothered or stressed by various externalities but more focused on your purpose. And lastly, purpose can actually help reduce inflammation. Inflammation in the body is heavily linked to cardiovascular disease and other degenerative diseases and is often brought on by stress.

A long life of purpose and well-being isn't just reserved for centenarians. A recent study in the U.S. found that people age 50 and older who had a strong sense of purpose in life were likely to live longer lives than their peers. The authors of the study believed that purposeful living gave these individuals the ability to better self-organize and have stimulating goals, all contributing to reducing risk factors for premature death. They "found a strong association between life purpose and mortality in the U.S." and pointed to evidence from a myriad of other studies across the world yielding similar results in relation to purpose and life longevity. In fact, in my own research of the world's leading studies on the drivers of well-being, purpose, or a life of meaning, showed up in nearly each and every study (see table).

Study	Factors of Well-Being		
Gallup: The Well Being Five	**Purpose** Social Financial	Physical Community	
The Organisation for Economic Co-operation and Development (OECD)	**Meaning and purpose** Autonomy	Competence	
Ryff Six Factors of Psychological Well-being	Self-acceptance Positive relations with others Autonomy	Environmental mastery **Purpose in life** Personal growth	
Seligman's PERMA Model of Well-being	Positive emotions Engagement Relationships	**Meaningful life (Purpose)** Accomplishment	
NIH Toolbox Emotional Assessment	Positive Affect Life Satisfaction	**Meaning & Purpose**	

At the end of the day, we all want to live a happy, healthy life, and purpose can go a long way in helping in that aim. What's crystal clear is that purpose is a key component of health and well-being. Some say that an apple a day keeps the doctor away. While there may or may not be some truth to that statement, one thing is for sure, knowing your purpose may be just what the doctor ordered for good health and a longer life.

PURPOSE FOR STRENGTH AND ENDURANCE

On September 11, 2016, George Chimel set off for a 3,000-mile trek to run from one end of the United States to the other. Mr. Chimel ended up running an average of 32 miles per day over a period of 92 days. So, I first had to pause to think about the gravity of what he had just accomplished. The first thought is how difficult it is to complete just ONE marathon. Mr. Chimel completed an equivalent of 120 marathons in roughly three months. While I find it personally staggering, Mr. Chimel had a purpose, and he had strength and endurance. He had strength and endurance from his purpose of raising awareness to Veterans of the United States Armed Forces.

You may want to ask yourself if your purpose is bigger than that adversity. We all have faced, are facing, or will face adversity, a storm of life that seems insurmountable that will take strength and endurance to overcome.

Imagine having to hike 10 miles in the cold rain, thunder, and lightning to get home. Waiting at home is your family and a fireplace and a nice big bowl of soup. Imagine that you are focused on the journey of making it home no matter what because there's nothing else that you want more in the world at that time, but the warmth of the fireplace, your family, and a hot bowl of soup. You encounter falls from the mud along the journey, deep cuts from the rocks and debris, and the chilly rain, lightning and thunder are all around you. You stay focused because you know that the purposeful journey is your only concern - to make it home. You fall, get up, and overcome the pain and fear you feel, and keep moving.

By the grace of God, you finally make it home. You are exhausted but feel a rush of energy because the love of your life wraps his or her warm body and arms around you. The warmth of the fireplace heals you. You sit down, and you eat that warm bowl of soup. How many of you have endured a storm to get home? Purpose is like home. It gives you mental, emotional, and even physical grounding, inspiration, and energy. You keep going, even in the storm.

SPIRITUAL ENDURANCE

The power of purpose can be drawn from spiritual endurance. Spiritual endurance comes from a belief that purpose is derived from the will of a higher power - from God. I had my awakening of spiritual purpose as I endured my own storm in 2013. As my marriage fell apart and I could not find a way to save it, I dug deeper into clarifying, solidifying, and walking in my purpose. I prayed to God to clarify my purpose and His will for my life. It felt like the warm home I had to journey towards through the wind, rain, thunder, and lightning. Along the journey, I had another storm to deal with - the frigid winter of job loss. After 18 years at the same company, I was given a pink slip. But I survived. No, in fact, I thrived.

My purpose had called me to a higher place while I felt like I was literally in the valley of the shadow of death. As a spiritual person and believer in God, I garnered strength and endurance through my belief in God and in His will and purpose for my life. My purpose had given me the strength to fight on, to believe with all of my being that I would one day hold the wisdom and character to be a light unto others, a light of purpose.

The Bible speaks of endurance, drawing upon God's power, saying, "train yourself to be Godly." This discipline is the active understanding that we must "run with endurance the race God has set before us." As I continued to draw strength from my spiritual purpose, my purpose met me where I was. I was once again employed, earned a Doctoral degree, and married the love of my life, all while in the storm. My purpose pulled me through and brought me to the other side.

Your purpose, too, has magnificence. Jim Rohn calls purpose a magnificent obsession. It is the magnificent obsession that pulls you to the future. It pulls you to the warm fireplace. It pulls you through all that you are going through, all kinds of challenges and difficulties. Your purpose pulls you through beyond today. The more clarity of purpose, the stronger it pulls. My purpose helped me find the strength and endurance to make it through the storm, and your purpose can help you.

PURPOSE FOR MAXIMIZED ENERGY

One of the greatest feelings in the world is when you open your eyes after a good night's sleep, think about the purposeful work that you are about to do, plant your feet firmly on the floor and enthusiastically jump out of bed ready to hit it. Bouncing out of bed ready for a purposeful day is rare in our society. Many of us simply want to stay in bed. We lay there and think to ourselves, "is it Friday yet?" Once we do get going and we start to move, that in turn begins to fuel our emotions, mental state and finally prepares us (after that hot cup of coffee) for our day.

What if we were energized from the top down, from our purpose? The book *The Power of Full Engagement* asserts that energy, and not time, is our most precious resource. According to the book's authors, Jim Loehr and Tony Schwartz, "the ultimate measure of our lives is not how much time we spend on the planet, but rather how much energy we invest in the time that we have." I would rephrase this to say, "how much (purposeful) energy we invest in the time we have." In other words, we want to maximize our energy in our own purposeful pursuits and not be driven by someone else's agenda or purpose.

The beauty of purpose is that it is indeed a source of energy. Purpose drives maximized energy and output in our lives. Energy is our collective fuel driven by a) physical energy; b) emotional connectedness; c) mental focus, and d) spiritual alignment. How we manage these four interconnected energy sources determines our overall engagement in life and whether we are invigorated, confident, joyful, connected, or depressed, exhausted, burned out, hopeless, and defeated.

Perhaps the strongest energy source known to man is spiritual. According to Loehr and Schwartz, "the most compelling source of purpose is spiritual, the energy derived from connecting to deeply held values and a purpose beyond one's self-interest." Spiritual energy has long been recognized as a powerful source of human inspiration, guidance, and influence. Spiritual energy moved great men and women like

Moses, Abraham, Jesus, Buddha, Mohammed, Mother Teresa, and Martin Luther King, Jr. to inspire great global change.

One of the greatest examples of spiritual energy as a driving force is that of Mahatma Gandhi. Gandhi believed that a natural attraction instinctively drives a person to sensory gratification and indulgence yet inherently seeks spiritual development in hopes of becoming our best selves. As a peaceful, non-violent leader of protests, Gandhi's life was a growth in his spiritually led purpose. According to Arvind Sharma, the author of the book *Gandhi: A Spiritual Biography*, Gandhi's life journey was a series of developmental steps described as a "spiritual-intellectual evolution" where he struggled with human limitations such as speaking up as a young lawyer. Gandhi would eventually elevate in his spiritual energy to focus on the concept of Satyagraha, or "insistence upon truth." This ideal formed the foundation of his life's purpose and work, garnering an enormous following of millions. Gandhi, who had been jailed by the British throughout the 1920s and early 1930s, announced in 1932 that he would "fast unto death" to protest British meddling in the new Indian constitution. Gandhi advocated his own peril for the "untouchables," considered as the lowest class of citizens in India, which he considered "Children of God."

Purpose provides the destination, the root source, and the ultimate goal for our energy and our lives. And while it provides a direction for our lives, it is also what "lights us up, floats our boats, and feeds our souls." In other words, purpose is power!

PURPOSE FOR LEADERSHIP AND BUSINESS

My purpose in life is to help people like you find your purpose and become your best self. Your best self is a life of mastery and means that you are the best leader of yourself, your family, your community, your business, and whatever domain to which you are obligated. The single most important factor in business is its *why*. In business terms, the why is the mission statement or statement of purpose - the reason for the existence of a business. I am of a strong belief that a business leader, or leader of any entity, be it a family, government, or other undertaking, must have a strong purpose in order to align, inspire and motivate employees, followers, and customers.

Steve Jobs, the founder of Apple, gave an interview in 2010 and was asked, "what do you imagine the next ten years of your life is going to be about?" He looked down to the floor, took a deep long breath, and paused to think. As he contemplated his answer, you could see a deep introspection in his gaze. He finally began to speak and said, "you know... when this whole thing with Gizmodo happened, I got a lot of advice from people who said 'you gotta just let it slide.' ...you shouldn't go after a journalist because they bought stolen property and they tried to extort you." He went on to say that "the worst thing that could happen is just to let it slide." Mr. Jobs explained that the core values and purpose of Apple did not change just because the company had grown larger and more popular. He reminded everyone that Apple "builds the best products in the world for people."

He further explained that nothing else makes his day more than receiving a random email from someone about how Apple's products are the coolest and greatest thing globally and how it positively affected their lives. At the end of the interview, he finally exclaimed, "that's what kept me going... It's what kept me going five years ago, ten years ago when the doors were almost closed, and it is what will keep me going five years from now, whatever happens."

Apple's mission reflects the personal purpose and mission of Steve Jobs, to make the best products in the world for people. Many of you reading this may own, and literally love, by the way, an iPhone, an iPad, or both. Steve Jobs was diagnosed with cancer in 2003 and passed away in October 2011, approximately a year after this interview. Steve Jobs was a great leader that led through a passionate purpose that literally kept the lights on at Apple so that the world would eventually purchase and adore over 2.2 billion iPhones as of November 2018.

Steve Jobs was the founder of Apple. He was the leader. The purpose and mission of Apple and his own purpose were the same. Leaders who have purpose give their followers and others a meaningful and passionate direction towards an ideal much larger than themselves. Steve Jobs certainly inspired an ideal much larger than himself that has impacted the world.

Purposeful leadership can drive a culture at your place of work beyond just profits. Purpose can be the fuel that engages employees to work for more than just a paycheck. Purposeful leaders inspire work cultures that drive meaning and engagement for their employees to build better products, deliver greater services, and drive greater value for customers. A recent study by LinkedIn revealed that workers who were driven from purpose had 64% higher rates of career fulfillment than those without a purposeful work environment.

Purposeful employees are better for the bottom line too. They are 20% more likely to stay longer with their company, which means there is less turnover. An organization's ability to retain employees reduces training costs, improves customer satisfaction, and generally leads to greater revenues. Purposeful leaders and organizations with a strong mission, vision, and values, are also more likely to entice purpose-oriented workers. In short, purposeful leaders attract purposeful workers and purposeful workers lead to profits.

The key to purposeful leadership is self-realization, understanding your strengths, weaknesses, values, passions, and self-actualization, understanding your purpose and mission in life, and leadership. The concept known as emotional intelligence (EQ) is "a set of emotional and social skills that influence the way we perceive and express ourselves, develop and maintain social relationships, cope with challenges, and use emotional information in an effective and meaningful way." The first building block of emotional intelligence is self-awareness and self-perception of which, self-actualization, also known as living with purpose, is the cornerstone. Put plainly, *if you wish to be an effective leader and motivate others to greatness and impact, you should be a purposeful leader.*

If you are a leader, to be most effective, you will need to align your purpose to the organization's purpose and clearly communicate your purpose to those you lead. This same concept applies to leaders of families, churches, community organizations, and other entities. Purposeful leadership can drive an enormity of benefits to you and those you lead.

A PURPOSEFUL LEGACY

I'd like you to think about your legacy. Your legacy is the memory of who you were after you die. It is the possessions, artifacts, stories, family values, and gifts that *you* leave behind. Legacy is the power of you now, hurled out in the future. For as much control as you have, you have the power to shape your legacy.

What legacy do you want to leave? Have you thought about the mark you want to leave after you die? Imagine yourself at 100 years old, surrounded by family at your deathbed. What would you like to think of your life, and how would you like those around you to think of you? This pattern of thinking relates to our values, our *terminal* values. Terminal values are our preferences for our end-states of existence. In other words, it is a reflection of what we ultimately care about at the end of our lives.

An article in Inc. Magazine explored the top 12 regrets people have before they die. Interestingly, the first four regrets had to do with character: 1) loving more, 2) worrying less, 3) forgiving more, and 4) having more courage. The fifth regret was wishing that they had lived their own life, exploring that business, changing careers, or having a family. In other words, that fifth regret is a regret of not having lived life on purpose. Ironically, the first four character values might be the key to accomplishing the fifth - loving what you do, not worrying about what others think, forgiving those along the journey, and having the courage to live out your purpose.

A strong legacy is aligned with a strong conviction of purpose. Think of three people who have died but have left a strong legacy. When you think of these people, what do you think of them? Do you think of their money? Or do you think of something deeper, perhaps how their purpose or core values in life has affected you personally?

You see, purpose promotes principles, values, and ultimately character. Our character is the outward expression of our deepest values and is based upon the tenets of life that one lives by no matter what the popular culture is saying. Our values and principles are inextricably linked to our purpose - they define who we are and manifest themselves in our core beliefs and actions, which define our legacy. King Solomon wrote, "A good person leaves an inheritance for their children's children, but a sinner's wealth is stored up for the righteous." In other words, a good person, someone of good character, values, principles, and purpose, leaves a lasting legacy beyond their days on earth, even extending to their grandchildren.

Yes, an inheritance of money has value, but an inheritance of purpose and character can be of even greater value. Knowing and living your purpose is like choosing to invest your money for future gains instead of spending the money on frivolous things today. Living with purpose and conviction of character can be challenging because it means choosing *not* to do certain things. Living with purpose can sometimes be a tough choice in the face of decisions that we can make that are gratifying in the moment.

An investment portfolio grows with what is called compound interest. Compound interest is simply interest payments on the interest payments. So as the interest "compounds," you see exponential growth in interest and thereby wealth. Living with purpose is the same way. Your purpose compounds to create exponential growth in your legacy. The stronger your conviction and action in your purpose, the stronger the likelihood that your legacy will live on as someone of great purpose, character, and conviction.

PART TWO

How to Find Your Purpose

CHAPTER 4

Finding Your Purpose Overview

"The meaning of life is to find your gift, the purpose of life is to give it away."
——*Pablo Picasso*——

    Can you recall old television shows and movies that had the plot of a pirate searching for buried treasure? The pirate, usually with a peg leg, an eye patch, and a trusty English-speaking parrot, sets out to find the treasure by using a treasure map. The map would always have an 'X' marking the spot where the treasure was buried. The adventure to find the treasure would be met with twists and turns and many challenges along the way. The treasure seeker would eventually discover the treasure after many painstaking trials and tribulations.

    Finding your purpose is a lot like hunting for buried treasure. There must be a deep desire to want to find your purpose - your treasure. There must be a path, a framework, or a map to help you find your purpose. For without it, just like the search for treasure, you may not even know where to look.

    In my research and reflection of my own life, I've determined a framework and map to find your purpose. The map and framework are simple yet can be challenging as it gives you a map to the most difficult treasure there is to find - the treasure of your why – your purpose. The framework to find your purpose is more of a circle, a continuum that allows you entry into it through one of three doorways: your story, your self-awareness, and your service to others.

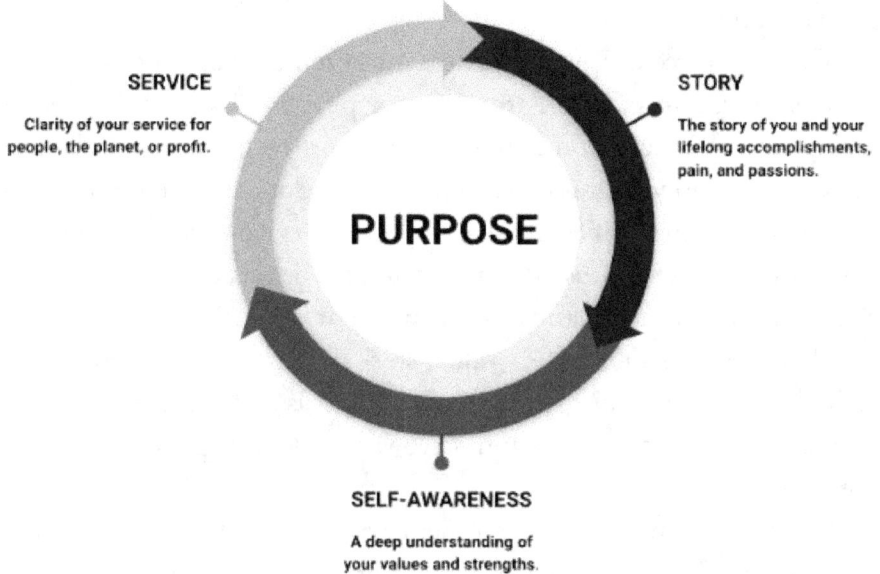

Your story is comprised of your life and your lifelong accomplishments. It is the culmination of your past self, the life milestones, themes, accomplishments, and setbacks. An examination and evaluation of your past is not a trap door that leads to stagnation but an unveiling that can lead to liberation in your life. This liberation is greater clarity of who you are, what makes you tick, and answering the bigger question - *why* you are.

Greater clarity of your story will serve as the onramp to greater self-awareness. Self-awareness gives you a greater understanding of your deepest values, strengths, competencies, and character. Self-awareness also unveils the person that you aspire to be, your best self. You will clarify the difference between the person you are now and the person you are becoming.

Service will give you clarity to a higher calling and the impact that you will have on the world. Purpose goes beyond just understanding yourself. It is a pull towards a meaningful mission and describes the impact you will have on planet earth in eternal space and time. It is your gift given to the world that so shines before men and women as a star unto the universe.

The next three chapters will dive into each of these doorways and help guide you to greater clarity of your purpose. I suggest following each chapter in succession as uncovering your story is the best place to understand who you are on a ground level. Your story feeds your self-awareness, which clarifies the major elements of your story into easily describable elements. It is like a raw diamond being cut into a wedding ring, clarifying its cut, clarity, carat, and color. As each of these "4 C's" can describe the stone and its value, so shall self-awareness clarify and fully describe your value to the world. For it is this value, your value, that gives service unto others and bestows the sweetest gift anyone could ever give - *you*.

Before continuing, take a moment or so to think about the statements below. This will give you greater awareness of your current state related to purpose while you are reading the next three chapters. There are no right or wrong answers.

- I have taken an inventory of my life to understand my personal life story.
- I have studied my family history and the impact it has had on who I am.
- I know what I am most passionate about in life.
- I have clarity on the root cause of negative emotions in my life.
- I can identify my deepest darkest challenges in my life.
- I know how those challenges have shaped the person I am today.
- I have clarity of the major themes of my life story.

- I can fully explain how my life story makes me who I am.
- I know my values, and I can easily articulate my top five.
- I have clarity of my strengths of skills and competencies.
- I know my levels of emotional intelligence.
- I have clarity of my character strengths.
- The work that I do has a major impact on people.
- I care about the planet and know exactly how to help it.
- My job allows me to contribute to the world in a significant way.

CHAPTER 5

Purpose Through the Power of Your Story

"There is no greater agony than bearing an untold story inside you."
—— *Maya Angelou* ——

My 3rd-grade teacher, Mrs. McVittie looked at me through her horn-rimmed glasses and said, "You will be back. You don't deserve to be with those kids." I have never forgotten those words. I was an eight-year-old boy who had gotten straight A's through the middle of my 3rd grade year. Although new to the school, I quickly became tapped as gifted and talented (GT) and selected to move to another class with the rest of the GT children. I recall having to pick up my desk to take it out of the door of Mrs. McVittie's class during the middle of the day. I walked in little steps not to hit the doorway with the desk. Perhaps it was foreshadowing or just plain meanness, but Mrs. McVittie's words seemed to pierce my mind and my soul, my eight-year-old self, absorbing those parting words like a sponge. "You will be back," rang over and over again in my head as I walked to my new class of GT children.

Those same words continued to reverberate in my head, like an echo in a horror movie. I walked to my new class, found a space for my desk *in the back*, and sat down. I was the new kid who did not belong here. I was afraid. I was afraid of my surroundings and afraid of failure. I remember finding a friend - at the back of the room. We were cool with one another and used to draw cars and trucks. We compared how good our drawings looked at the expense of paying attention to the teacher. In a week or so, "I was back." I was back in Mrs. McVittie's class.

I have always struggled with the feeling of not being good enough. Am I good enough? This question has haunted me since the day I was told by my 3rd-grade teacher that I was not. This feeling has been with me well into adulthood. I now know that not only am I good enough, but that I can help other gifted and talented people discover that they are good enough too.

My story unlocked the realities of the root cause of my fears, pain, passion, strengths, and challenges. The story of Mrs. McVittie, a part of my story, helps to explain how a painful situation as a young child can be the catalyst for my belief system. I believed that I was not good enough to be in the GT class. But I now know that I have a love of learning that predates "McVittie-gate" and has been a key component of my purpose discovery.

I didn't know that this early life episode would develop into a pattern of feeling not good enough when I am "in the room" of other GT-like people. There have been plenty of times that I have led or been in meetings with high-caliber executives where the scene would play out in my head, "you'll be back." Those words would often hold me captive to my feelings of insecurity and have been a major part of my story. But with any good story, there is a pattern of events that culminates in a resolution to the conflict, challenge, or barrier, giving the main character of the story victory and a life lesson. A moral lesson that helps shape his character and further builds the hero's strength gives way to growth and clarity of purpose as to why he even exist.

Part of my purpose was to realize that no matter what someone else thought of me, especially if that person was held responsible for teaching, mentoring, and molding me, I would keep a healthy belief in myself. I found out that I would continue to hold my head high, upright, and be steadfast in the face of challenges. I found out that I would keep my back straight in the face of adversity, set my shoulders, and always believe with all of my mind, heart, and soul that I "belong in the room."

THE POWER OF STORIES

Stories have been a powerful tool for communication among human beings for thousands of years. As long as there have been humans on earth with language, there have been stories that have been told. These stories have passed along to family, community, and cultural norms, patterns, and belief systems over centuries.

Stories hold both the information and emotional insights from the experiences of others. I imagine that you hold many memories - stories - from your childhood, both good and bad. Many of those stories hold life lessons and have helped shape who you are and what you care deeply about.

Brain science points to reasons why stories are so powerful. Stories are a powerful means of communicating which bolsters our ability to capture information both rationally and emotionally. Three neurological responses occur which elicit strong emotions from a good story:

1. Stress Response - Tense moments of the story, particularly related to the rising action and climax, produces the stress hormone cortisol, which focuses on the story.
2. "Cute Factor" Response - There is a release of oxytocin, also known as the "feel good" chemical, which promotes empathy and connection when something "cute" is a part of the story (like babies and puppies).
3. Reward Response - A happy ending to a story triggers the limbic system, our brain's reward center, releasing dopamine, which makes us feel encouraged, optimistic, and hopeful.

As you can see, the brain's response to a good story is enormously powerful. And yes, that is the same dopamine that you have heard about associated with the feeling you get from drug use or gambling. These emotional responses also lead to enhancements in memory. Think for a moment about the most precious and memorable parts of your life. You most likely remember the stories related to good or bad times. Moments in your life of achievement and reward are most likely linked to the reward response. Moments of challenge or pain in your life most likely elicited the stress response. These neurological responses also increase the memory of these stories by anchoring in the parts of the brain responsible for our emotions.

Stories can provide a powerful means to the discovery and even clarity of your purpose. Purpose can be found in the pain, challenges, and problems of your past. Sayings like "pressure makes diamonds" and "tough people are made in hard places" serve up truth as the purposes of many have been created and sharpened through the most excruciating of circumstances. A diamond, perhaps recognized as the earth's most precious element beyond life itself, takes approximately 1 to 3.3 billion years to form at immense pressures within the depths of the earth at temperatures of greater than 2000 degrees Fahrenheit (1050 degrees Celsius). Sometimes the most brilliant existence can take years to form in the hottest, toughest, and most challenging of environments.

HOW STORIES LEAD TO PURPOSE

On August 28, 1955, a young 14-year-old boy named Emmett Till was brutally murdered. A young Till was murdered for being accused of offending a white woman working in her family's grocery store. His mother, Mamie Till, decided to use the power of Emmett's story to make a difference in the world. Mamie Till decided that in order to tell Emmett's story best, she would keep an open casket at his funeral for the world to watch and see. The bloated, disfigured, and mangled body of Emmett Till laying in the casket was shown on the front pages of newspapers and magazines across the country. Emmett Till's story would be told to the world and told in a most visually stunning and powerful way.

As painful as the story was, it drove Mamie Till's purpose for the rest of her life. It drove her light and her decision to show the open casket at Emmett's funeral. In fact, this story changed the course of human history. This one act of courage and purpose catalyzed a bus boycott in Alabama 100 days later. The residents of Alabama had seen enough. The bus boycott was planned, but it needed a leader. That need sparked a call to a young 26-year-old preacher named Dr. Martin Luther King Jr. to come to Alabama to lead the boycott. The bus boycott thrust a young Dr. King into the national spotlight, which many say was the inception of what has become to be known as the Civil Rights Movement. It was Mamie Till's telling of a tragic story, a mother's pain beyond words, that sparked her purpose, which became the light that sparked a revolution.

PASSION, PAIN & PROMOTION

Passion has become a term that is often used synonymously with purpose. I love the word passion and believe that it is a key ingredient to purpose. Passion can be known as the one thing you love to do in life and what you want to become in life. It might be the dream of being an astronaut, a singer, or actor you had as a child. Purpose is when passion meets your strengths (understood from self-awareness) and what the world needs (your service). Passion is discovered through the fullness of your story, both the good and the bad. Passion can be formed through two realities of your story - pain or promotion.

Pain is often experienced from tragedies or challenging events in our lives. Harrison Monarth, an executive communications coach, describes the use of pain for helping his clients find their passion this way:

> *"I am asking them to revisit times of great personal pain. But as they recount their experiences, they begin to see that they are also returning to moments of greatness. Our painful experiences often bring out our best selves. Recalling the lessons of such moments releases positive emotions and makes it easier to see what's possible in the present."*

Our pain produces moments of greatness when we find out who we truly are and what we are truly passionate about. Mamie Till's pain fueled her passion and, ultimately, her purpose in life. Pain fuels greatness. But fortunately for us, pain is not the only factor in fueling passion or greatness.

The other input to passion is something that you are great at doing, where you have been promoted in life. Think of a time in your life when you were rewarded for a job well done. Think of a time where you used your gifts and talents to do something great, where you stood above your peers. Promotion can be a powerful tool for discovering your passion and your purpose. The more clarity you have of the story surrounding your passion, the better you can harness its power. The key to gaining clarity of your passion is through reflecting on and telling your story.

THE COMPONENTS OF YOUR STORY

Stories and storytelling generally follow a similar pattern of an introduction, middle, and an end. One of the most used and popularized structures for storytelling is what is known as Freytag's Pyramid. The Pyramid consists of five main elements: a) introduction, b) rise, c) climax, d) return or fall, and e) catastrophe or outcome.

The 5 Elements of Freytag's Pyramid

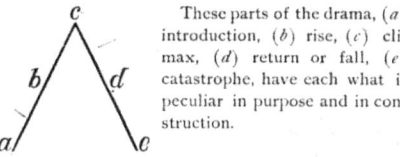

These parts of the drama, (*a*) introduction, (*b*) rise, (*c*) climax, (*d*) return or fall, (*e*) catastrophe, have each what is peculiar in purpose and in construction.

Freytag's framework can serve as a basis for uncovering and telling your story. I like the addition of an overall theme or moral of a story. Life is full of opportunities to gain wisdom, knowledge, and understanding so that we may learn from the stories of our lives. I suggest four main groupings, combining key elements when uncovering your story:

1. **Introduction** - The introduction provides an opportunity for you to reveal who you are, the time period, the place, or the location. It also provides an opportunity to reveal a "complication" or challenge that you are dealing with.
2. **Rising Moment & Climax** - This part of the story represents the movement towards an inflection point, where things either a) fall apart or b) start improving. It represents the fullest energy of the story where something big happens. This is the most important part of the story.
3. **Falling Action & Conclusion** - The falling action represents the part of the story where things either a) improve or b) move further toward destruction. The conclusion reveals the final triumph or catastrophe. Here, it describes the resolution, the joy achieved in the arc of the story, or the character's ultimate undoing.
4. **Theme & Moral** - The theme, or the moral of the story, is discovered and revealed. What did you learn about yourself? What did you learn about the world? What was the main takeaway from the story? These questions form the basis of the key theme or moral of the story.

These four areas can combine to tell a compelling story. The theme and moral of the story provide key takeaways that make us our best selves. We learn from our mistakes, and we embed our triumphs in our self-identity and self-regard.

THE BOURNE IDENTITY

The story framework can help you discover and compellingly tell your own story and clarify your purpose. Your story consists of many episodes or short stories, as well as an overarching life story. I often use a technique called "The Bourne Identity" with my coaching and leadership training clients to help uncover their story, often decade by decade or as a reflection of a significant period in their lives.

In the movie, The Bourne Identity, Jason Bourne (Matt Damon) awakens, salvaged, and near death in the ocean by a fishing boat. When he recuperates, Mr. Bourne suffers from total amnesia and has no identity or knowledge of his background. However, he has a set of extraordinary talents and skills in language, fighting, and self-defense. He sets out on a desperate search to discover his past and uncover the truth about his identity, all the while being chased by deadly assassins who seek to take his life.

Hopefully, you are not in this dire situation, but the search for meaning and clarity of your past can be powerful. I would like you to do The Bourne Identity Exercise. In this exercise, your instructions are to search through each decade of your life (or a significant time period) and think of the major events, moments, and milestones in your life that had a major impact on you and your development as a person.

I used my own life experience in the example below. I chose the timeframe of 10 – 18 years old and talked about my experiences that follow an arc from childhood challenges to unstable friendships and overcoming obstacles towards a brighter future.

Table - Example of The Bourne Identity Exercise

Time Frame	Introduction	Rising Moment / Climax	Falling Action / Conclusion	Theme / Moral of the Story
10 - 18	I was moving a lot as a child. I moved every year from the age of 10 to 18. I moved from Tennessee to Texas, to Maryland, to Virginia during this time. I lived with my mom and didn't know my dad.	I always felt like I didn't fit in with the other kids but could find my footing with friends when I turned 13. Unfortunately, we moved again, every year and I lacked identity and close friends. I found myself at a turning point in high school, hanging out with a wild bunch, often getting in fights, and being rebellious.	I became a really good gymnast. I straddled the line between personal destruction and growing into a better person who could go to college. I became an All-American Gymnast winning multiple awards. I got better grades my junior and senior year of high school and received a scholarship to James Madison University.	I learned that hard work paid off and that loving something that I was good at (gymnastics) could pave the way to a brighter future. I was the first person in my family to go to college and gain confidence for life that I could accomplish anything. **Theme** – Great things are possible for me despite life challenges

Take some time to figure out your Bourne Identity using the chart in the appendix. You can also get a copy to download at www.anthonyperdue.com/purposetopower.

Here are some additional questions to help you think through the exercise:

- What were your proudest moments as a child, teenager, and adult?
- What were the most devastating events in your life? What led up to it, how did it happen, and what was the result?
- What made you happy? Be as specific as possible, reflecting on the events or relationships with others that triggered your emotions.
- What were values consistently framed by your parents or the people you were around who raised you? What were the stories surrounding how the values were imparted to you?
- What events made you cry, and what effect did that have on you?
- What long-standing values, beliefs, and lessons learned did you develop during your decades, and why?
- What strengths did you develop, how and when? Also, think of the things that you accomplished that were attached to your gifts and talents.

Culminate these answers into stories during specific time frames, either decades or groupings over the years. Feel free to get specific at a particular time (1 - 2 years) if that will help you better understand your story. Upon completion, you should have anywhere from 5 - 10 short stories of your life. The key here is to unearth key themes from each time frame in your life. Each story of a timeframe in your life should have a moral or a key theme that you've learned from and have even lived by. This helps define who you are and those major times in your life that contributed to that definition.

I would encourage you to connect or reconnect with people that were the main characters in your story during that time of your life. Observers of our actions and moments in life can often give us more objective clarity of ourselves from the outside looking in. You can also ask them many of the questions listed above and what they observed about you during those time frames.

We are going to use these stories to create greater self-awareness, which is the next step for finding your purpose. I encourage you to take some time to reflect upon and write down your stories before moving on. I believe it will be well worth your time.

Key takeaways

- Stories are a powerful means of communicating which bolsters our ability to capture information both rationally and emotionally.
- The term passion is a term that is often used synonymously with purpose. However, passion is an emotional response formed through realities of pain or promotion.
- Freytag's framework can serve as a basis for uncovering and telling your story.
- The Bourne Identity Exercise can help you uncover your own life story and provide the building block to greater self-awareness.

CHAPTER 6

Purpose Through Self-Awareness

"Your own Self-Realization is the greatest service you can render the world."
——*Ramana Maharshi*——

The journey to finding your purpose begins with self-awareness. You must become self-aware to understand and, more importantly, deeply believe and desire to live in your purpose. You must know yourself, in order to become yourself. As you will discover, purpose is driven from within. It is driven by the elements that make you, you. You are defined by your thoughts, feelings, wants, needs, desires, motivations, will, and actions. All that you are shows up on stage to yourself and to the world.

Becoming self-aware is the foundation for unlocking your life's mission and purpose. But the challenge is in actually becoming self-aware. Your story goes a long way towards self-awareness, but more work must be done. Self-awareness is a challenging topic because it usually involves taking a deeper look at who you are. Some, if not most of us, may not always like what we see or what we have seen. You may have some skeletons that you wish to keep buried deep in that closet forever. Those same skeletons may just be your deliverance to your purpose.

Your story was the first step in unlocking the depths of who you are. But the work to dig deeper begins. This chapter is extremely important in launching the inward journey to yourself, your future, and your legacy. It may require some deep digging into your soul's soil to gain access to the roots. As with any tree, the roots provide the strength, fortitude, and direction of the growth. Self-awareness gives you access to the roots. It exposes your strengths and weaknesses, the good, the bad, and the ugly. Embrace the digging process within you.

Many of us just go through life accepting what comes at us and responding at the moment. We often live our lives as a call and response. Have you ever been to an old-school hip-hop concert? The MC (master of ceremonies) will do his or her best job to get the crowd hyped by saying, "tell me where y'all from." Without even thinking, the crowd yells back, "Maryland," or whatever state, city, or area you represent. Or even more surprising, the MC will say something like, "throw your hands in the air, and wave them like you just don't care!" The reaction becomes one that is physical as hands go up in the air and wave side to side in unison to the beat.

This call and response are the same things that we often do daily. We are called by social media, called by advertising, called by our routines, and called by whatever responsibilities are being determined by the MC. The MC often represents the agendas, mandates, and motives of others - usually costing you time, money, or other precious resources.

But how often do you stop and self-reflect? How often do you sit quietly and think about your motives, thoughts, feelings, strengths, weaknesses, desires, and drives? What is the call inside your heart and soul, begging for your purposeful response? Who's your favorite MC? Is it you, or is it someone or something else? You see, our ability to self-reflect and respond to our own call opens the window into our own mind, heart, and soul. Stephen Covey calls this the circle of concern. Are you concerned within your circle or outside of your circle?

Your story helps to unlock the past and the keys to open the door to self-awareness. Self-awareness leads to self-realization where you reflect on, understand, and have a deep desire to become your best self, your realized self in the present. Self-realization is where you become not only aware of yourself, gain clarity of your past and your present, but it gives you a window into your future self. More importantly, it gives you a window into the process of becoming your future self. As the window becomes clear, devoid of steam, dirt, and haziness - the process, the journey, and the mission to your destiny become clear. That clarity will provide the energy, fuel, and internal motivation to be what you see. As we begin this journey, let's take a deeper look at self-awareness and self-reflection as it relates to purpose.

WHAT IS SELF-AWARENESS?

γνῶθι σεαυτόν

The definition of the Greek term above is to "know thyself." It is a famous saying often attributed to Plato or Socrates that has been said to have been written at the ancient Greek ruins of the Temple of Apollo at Delphi. Philosophers spent their lives seeking to find out what it means to "know thyself."

The topic of self-awareness is certainly not new and has been studied throughout the centuries as early as 600 BC in India and 500 BC in China. Self-awareness can be considered many things. There are almost countless ways to think about and view self-awareness, from states of mind, thinking, feeling, acting, your values, and knowing and understanding our strengths and weaknesses.

UNCOVERING SELF-AWARENESS

From a psychological and philosophical perspective, self-awareness boils down to two interrelated perspectives; *reflective* self-awareness and *objective* self-awareness. In other words, we can fully uncover self-awareness from two main sources, 1) our own self-reflection and 2) the observations of others.

REFLECTIVE SELF-AWARENESS

The first perspective focuses on our capacity to become the object of our own reflection, focusing on our internal workings of thought, feelings, and desires. This is our ability to assess ourselves from various angles and various levels of consciousness. The concept of consciousness is both simple and challenging in understanding self-awareness. On the one hand, it is simple. After all, we can think of ourselves as conscious because we just know we are. On the other hand, challenging because the level of consciousness or awareness differs by individual.

We are generally in four levels of consciousness or awareness:

1. Unconsciousness - This is a state where there is no processing of information from either the self or environment. Examples of this include coma and sleep.
2. Consciousness - This is where we can think, perceive, experience sensations but are unaware that these events are taking place. Human beings spend much time in a state of consciousness, interacting with objects and people, talking, walking, and thinking.
3. Self-Awareness - This refers to the capacity to become the object of one's own attention. We become a reflective observer, processing self-information. This awareness can be focused on the experience of specific thoughts of life and mental events, behaviors, along with the possession of unique characteristics (expressions of beliefs and values). We verbalize thoughts, feelings, and actions with phrases like a) I am good. I am creative. I am intelligent; b) I feel tired, and I look good. I am walking confidently. This level of awareness is achievable but takes reflection, effort, and practice.
4. Meta Self-Awareness - This is the state of being aware that one is self-aware. You could vocalize that "I'm aware of the fact that I'm angry" or "I'm currently analyzing my emotional state of feeling angry." This aligns strongly with the definition of self-awareness as related to emotional awareness, also known as emotional intel-

ligence. Meta self-awareness allows us to reflect upon and understand the triggers of emotions while having the ability to have a planned response.

To graduate within the four levels of self-awareness, it is critical that we reflect on how we think, feel, and act, as well as observe and understand the characteristics of who we are. Understanding how we show up in thought, emotion, and action allows us to better understand our purpose and how our purposeful journey can play out moment to moment. The good news is that we are not alone in our observations of ourselves, and we have the opportunity to gain insights into ourselves through the eyes of others.

OBJECTIVE SELF-AWARENESS

Have you ever received feedback from a boss or co-worker? If so, think about that feedback right now. Was it good? Was it productive? Did you agree or disagree with the feedback? How did you respond both in the moment and after some time to the feedback? Typically, feedback given on the job is in alignment with a standard of work. This standard is a determined state or way of conducting your work in order to be a productive employee. Objective self-awareness is the process of self-reflection and assessment against a standard of performance for behavior, progress, or outcomes.

Objective self-awareness can be a powerful way to approach self-awareness because you are not simply relying on your own view of yourself. Self-awareness that is based solely upon one's self-reflection can be flawed. It has been said that 96% of us lie. We lie to ourselves. We lie to others, and, more often than not, we are unaware of this challenge. One way to ensure that we are not lying to ourselves is through the reflection and congruence of others' observations and self-awareness.

Congruence is the alignment of your self-awareness (reflective) with those that assess your skills, traits, emotions, and states of being (objective). This is not to say that it is impossible to gain greater self-awareness alone, however, research suggests that self-awareness in alignment with others' assessment of you will yield greater accuracy. According to Ashley and Reiter-Palmon, those whose self-assessment aligned with others have higher performance levels than those who are not aligned with their assessors.

As an example, I recently gave a presentation and training on authentic leadership to a group of executives. After the discussion had concluded, one of the participants approached me and said, "man, you were really in your element up there. It was like that is exactly what you should be doing." I thanked him, of course, and began to self-reflect about the feedback I had just received. We all need words of affirmation and encouragement in our lives and that moment was indeed encouraging for me, as I believe that when I am training a group of executives, I am indeed walking in my purpose. This greater self-awareness will improve your ability to more accurately determine your purpose and have more clarity, confidence, and effectiveness in carrying out your purpose.

THE CHALLENGES OF SELF-AWARENESS

The shadows of your past hold your future hostage.

I have a confession to make. I love the show, South Park. As crude and unbecoming as it is, I just love the show. I especially love watching Erik Cartman and his shenanigans. In one of the episodes, Cartman, as he's not so affectionately known, was lured to a cabin by all of his friends. While wearing a t-shirt that says, "Token's Life Matters," Cartman begins to pull out all of his video games on the table while his entire crew of young boys are surrounding him with the intention of destroying his entire collection of video games and he is none the wiser. The boys, especially Token, approach Cartman and begin stabbing and destroying all of his equipment while Cartman begs and screams for them to stop. Cartman eventually falls to the floor and passes out from the agony of his friends destroying his video games, iPad, iPhone, and all of his equipment.

While I would imagine that this has not happened to you, the point here is that Cartman just wanted to play video games. He was totally unaware of his behavior and actions that caused his entire crew of so-called friends to destroy his stuff. While this example is extreme (and hilarious to some), it does represent how we can oftentimes lack self-awareness.

There are many reasons why we lack self-awareness:

- We don't think about it
- We don't think it's important
- We don't know how we feel
- We aren't aware of what others think or feel about us
- We don't know our strengths or weaknesses
- We are not aware of our values or beliefs
- We are not aware of our emotional triggers (what set's us off)
- We are unaware of our abilities in comparison to a standard
- We don't have a 'to be' state of being (purpose & vision)
- We don't practice self-reflection
- It is damaging to our sense of self (especially our weaknesses)

So while there can be many causes of lack of self-awareness, the key is to truly understand why. In engineering, there is a concept known as the "five whys." This technique is used to get to the root cause of engineering issues and problems. So our problem is to understand the cause of any challenge to our self-awareness. What is the root cause contributing to a lack of self-awareness? On the surface, one could easily say, "I just haven't focused on it." While this might be true, there may in fact be reasons holding you back from achieving self-awareness or even meta self-awareness (as described in Morin's four-stage self-awareness model above).

REFLECTION VS. RUMINATION

There are generally two states of mind when approaching self-awareness - positive and negative. It's almost as simple as reflecting on the good or the bad, God or evil, and positive and negative. Reflection can be a powerful way to unlock a deeper understanding of ourselves, leading to a more clear path to our purpose. The challenge is that not all reflection is positive reflection. We can reflect on the good and bad in a positive way. We can examine who we are, both the rose petals and the thorns, and gain a full 360-degree view of ourselves without developing a negative perception of ourselves.

That said, our ability to self-reflect and thus become self-aware could be limited by our own need to protect ourselves. We often inflate our perceptions of ourselves to protect our self-esteem and begin to enhance and inflate our self-image. In other words, many of us possess a bias towards inflating who we are to protect ourselves from negative feelings about ourselves. Research suggests two ways people engage in self-focus: self-reflection and self-rumination, which can help us understand which lens, be it positive or negative, that we see ourselves.

Reflection

Reflection is our ability to think about ourselves or the self as perceived by others. This reflection can represent the past, present, and future, also known as the grounded self, true self, and possible self. We reflect on a combination of our self-images of the past, the present, and the future. Mark Manson asserts that we should only reflect on the negative perceptions to free ourselves from "caring" for what we lack. However, it is possible to reflect on the positive and the negative, but with a positive mindset.

Positive reflection is when a self-aware person can find self-acceptance from within for both the positive and the negative. It is the ability to accept our faults and bad traits and not be surprised or defensive when we hear criticism or feedback. But what about being positive when we reflect on something that we lack? Is it possible that we can reflect against a standard that we do not possess and remain positive? For example, I'd personally like to lose 20 pounds. Should I feel bad about myself because I am not a supermodel with 10% body fat? The answer is no. I can accept this reality without feeling too bad about myself or exacerbating feelings of negativity towards myself.

Rumination

Take a few seconds and think about what you do well. Some of us are great at learning, creating, strategic thinking, organizing, teaching, cooking, relating to others, and executing, to name a few. We also have anxieties and fears in life, from bees, snakes, heights, doctors (e.g., white coat syndrome), speaking in front of an audience, etc. These negative thoughts and anxieties can leave us paralyzed, just from the thought of the subject itself, without even going through the experience.

These negative thoughts, anxieties, and images of ourselves are what is known as rumination. Rumination is where anxious attention is paid to ourselves, and we ruminate over the negative, focusing on negative thoughts of fear, failure, and self-worth. Rumination is associated with anxiety and depression and can negatively affect how we feel about ourselves. The challenge here is to be able to self-reflect and not self-ruminate. So what about those 20 pounds? I maintain that I can be happy with who I am in my current state while positively striving toward my 20-pound goals. That gap is not a gap of pain but a gap of purpose. I can reflect on my current weight while reflecting on my goal of losing 20 pounds and maintaining a positive outlook on life.

Rumination can be dangerous because it can block us from our purpose. If our negative thoughts about ourselves become real enough to keep us from taking action, it can be like a flower planted below a shadow that never gets enough sunlight to go into full bloom. Rumination can be this shadow, and the shadow can block self-awareness. If we ruminate and think the worst about ourselves, we often protect ourselves from the pain of negative thoughts through defensiveness, deception, and dissonance.

The first response is what is known as defensiveness. Defensiveness is when we try to deny or counter criticisms or feedback in areas of our lives where we are sensitive. Being defensive can become so built-in that it can become an automatic response initiating our "fight or flight" coping mechanism in our brains. Being defensive can lead to challenges of our emotions, including anger, anxiety, and even a lack of empathy towards others. Have you ever found yourself "clapping back" or responding harshly to someone attempting to give you positive feedback? If so, you may have this challenge.

The key to overcoming defensiveness is, first and foremost, self-forgiveness and self-acceptance. Self-forgiveness and self-acceptance can unlock the door to self-love and compassion, where we sustain a positive reflection of ourselves even in our mess.

The second response is self-deception. We often deceive ourselves because of some underlying motivation associated with self-protection. Psychologist Neel Burton refers to self-deception as "unconscious processes that we deploy to diffuse the fear and anxiety that arise when we think we are or who we think we should be."

According to the Stanford Encyclopedia of Philosophy, "self-deception involves a person who seems to acquire and maintain some false belief." The simple definition is that we lie to ourselves. However, what is also known is that we are often unaware that we are deceiving ourselves. In other words, our unawareness hinders our ability to be self-aware. It is a closed feedback loop within ourselves. Our journey of *Purpose to Power* is not to deceive ourselves but to expose ourselves to ourselves to become the best versions of ourselves.

The third area is what is known as cognitive dissonance. As bad as defensiveness and self-deception are, cognitive dissonance can be even more damaging to our self-awareness. When confronted with information that challenges or contradicts their beliefs, cognitive dissonance is where people are thrown into negative feelings that cause them to either rationalize or justify their misperceptions. In other words, you may end up doing something that goes against what you know to be the right thing to do. Cognitive dissonance can be especially damaging because we are often aware that our behavior is misaligned with our beliefs. So, we may be self-aware of our actions, but that misalignment with our beliefs can cause extreme discomfort and pain. Confronting ourselves with our own self-awareness can be challenging, so we can either a) change the behavior to align with beliefs, b) change or attempt to change our beliefs, or c) reduce the importance of those beliefs.

To walk in full purpose and power requires that we try our best to align our actions with our beliefs. This can be difficult, however, prioritizing our positive beliefs and purpose can lead to a life of fulfillment. Steven Covey once said, "The successful person has the habit of doing things failures don't like to do. They don't like doing them either, necessarily. But their disliking is subordinated to the strength of their purpose." Whether it is defensiveness, self-deception, or cognitive dissonance, I believe the exploration of self-awareness and the journey of purpose and power will help you overcome these potential challenges in your life.

I wanted to give you a full understanding of self-awareness to have a deeper understanding of engaging in your own self-awareness, avoiding the pitfalls of rumination, defensiveness, deception, and dissonance. Our ability to reflect and gain feedback from others determines our ability to become self-aware and clarify our purpose in life.

In the next chapters, we will explore the three key elements of self-awareness that are the most foundational for understanding purpose - 1) your values, 2) your strengths, and 3) your emotional self-awareness.

THE THREE COMPONENTS OF SELF-AWARENESS

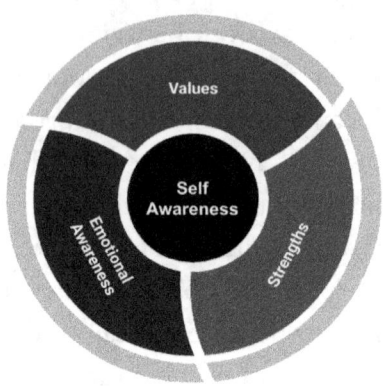

Key takeaways

- Self-awareness is the key to uncovering self-realization and the journey to your future self of purpose.
- Self-awareness has been studied for centuries and reflects our thinking, feeling, acting, values, and understanding our strengths and weaknesses.
- Self-awareness boils down to two interrelated perspectives; *reflective* self-awareness and *objective* self-awareness.
- Challenges to self-awareness include rumination, defensiveness, deception, and dissonance.
- The building blocks of self-awareness for purpose discovery are your values, strengths, and emotional self-awareness.

CHAPTER 7

Self-Awareness Through Values

"When your values are clear to you, making decisions becomes easier."
——*Roy Disney*——

Values are *the* key ingredient in self-awareness and purpose discovery. Our values serve as critical components of our being because they often guide what we do without our knowing. Values reflect what is important to us in life and drive the development of strategies and priorities used to make key decisions when evaluating tradeoffs.

Our choices are based on values that serve to meet our needs. Abraham Maslow was a world-renowned psychologist who proposed that human beings have a specific set of needs that can be arranged in what has come to be known as Maslow's hierarchy of needs. Maslow asserted that "people have physiological, safety, social, esteem, and self-actualization needs." According to Maslow, once a person's basic needs are met (physiological, safety, and social), they focus on their higher-level needs (esteem and self-actualization).

Our various needs create a dilemma of competing choices for each of us. Hultman and Gellerman discuss the dilemma this presents this way:

> *"This dilemma places us between two sets of forces: those pulling toward safety and those pushing toward growth and development... How people resolve this dilemma depends on their values... every action is guided by one or more values."*

Our values determine which needs will win the competition, growth, and development, or safety and security. Values shape how we satisfy our needs through action. Maslow goes further, however, and describes how our values can either progress us into our preferred (future) self or inhibit growth altogether:

> *"Maslow (1968) distinguished three types of values: growth values, "coasting" values (healthy regression), and defensive values (unhealthy regression). He maintained that people have a natural desire for growth, but they need homeostatic values for peace, rest, and relaxation. He asserted that more mature and healthy people place greater emphasis on growth but that "coasting" values are always necessary. Defensive values protect against pain, fear, loss, and threat, but they can significantly inhibit growth."*

These three types of values: growth, coasting, and defensive, define who we are. These groups of values are the linchpin to self-awareness because they address our basic human needs. They determine who we are and how we show up when faced with choices in life that represent the full spectrum of what we need, want, and desire. Human beings are usually a combination of the three types of values, with a primary focus on one type:

- Defensive - I primarily seek to maintain my self-esteem.

- Coasting (stabilizing) - I primarily seek to maintain things as they are.
- Growth - I primarily seek to self-actualize (to become my best self)

While there are three types of values, I would argue that our values' true result manifests in defensive values or growth values. There is an old saying that you are either growing or dying. There is no middle ground. In other words, unless there is growth, there is death. You either live your life through growth values, which aspire to a higher form of self or die through your defensive values, which defend who you already claim to be. The reason for this is because of the movement of the world.

The world waits on no man or woman. Our society, be it in politics, the environment, the culture, technology, the legal system, economics, etc., is always changing. It is always progressing forward - growing in some way. Therefore, if you are coasting and primarily focused on maintaining things as they are, you are, in fact, not maintaining anything because the world is passing you by, and you are ultimately dying. Your desire for stability will be in vain if there is not enough focus on growth, and you will ultimately align more with values that are defensive in nature.

DEFENSIVE VALUES VS. GROWTH VALUES

While defensive values are not always necessarily bad and growth values good, the main problem with defensive values is that they usually function to protect self-esteem from being lowered. While it is wise to be cautious, safe, and defensive to guard against manipulation or control, people who emphasize defensive values invest their energy in preventing bad things from happening rather than making good things happen. They spend a large portion of their lives seeking reassurance and encouragement from others.

While this may not seem problematic on the surface, continuous efforts to prevent a negative inhibit efforts to grow positively. Because of this, basic needs for growth (Self-actualization) remain largely unsatisfied. This is why overly defensive people fail to find and sustain true happiness and satisfaction. Their negative conceptions of themselves and others are almost always causal factors in personal, interpersonal team, and organizational problems. The table below gives examples of growth and defensive values.

GROWTH VERSUS DEFENSIVE VALUES

Growth Values	Defensive Values
Adaptability	Caution
Affirmation	Clean
Authenticity	Independence
Acceptance	Logical
Creativity	Material possessions
Empowerment	Security
Commitment	Speed
Collaboration	Winning
Excellence	Competition
Giving	Control
Faith	Power
Inclusiveness	Prestige
Innovation	Self-interest
Knowledge	Seniority
Love	Expediency
Optimism	Manipulation
Perseverance	Obedience
Quality	Self-control
Service	Approval
Social Awareness	Courtesy
Spirituality	Loyalty
Stewardship	Status
Teamwork	Territory
Truth	Tact

GROWTH VALUES

A focus on growth and growth values can guide you towards achieving your potential across various areas, including creativity, innovation, knowledge, flexibility, trust, and integrity (see table above). Values such as integrity, respect for others, gratitude, excellence, service, and self-care drive our purpose and become a significant energy source, especially when they move from negative to positive in our lives.

While you may not already live in the fullness of specific growth values, it is the desire to progress towards the realization of truly walking in the aspired value or values that matter most. There is transformative value in the growth values themselves, which guides us to a higher place. You might not be where you want to be, but you can say to yourself, "I aspire to walk in the fullness of values of love, trust, creativity, and spirituality to reflect the fullness and purpose for who I am."

The process of reflecting your transformed self into the future is the core of self-development. This process is known as individuation, or self-realization. In other words, we can aspire towards living out higher values to become the best and highest version of ourselves. The Greeks called this concept Arete, or excellence of self through character and competency development. They focused on virtues, aka values, and put forth the philosophy that by understanding and living virtuous lives, or understanding our values and living them, we would experience our 'best life.'

This topic, in modern terms, is known as subjective well-being. It is a belief born through positive psychology that we can flourish and become our happiest if we understand and live our values and focus on our values' strengths. I encourage you to define those values and beliefs that are most important to you. These values will be foundational to finding your purpose and living with power. Take a few minutes to complete the values exercise below.

THE TOP FIVE VALUES EXERCISE

This exercise aims to help you identify the values that are the most important to you to help inform you of your purpose. Take about five to ten minutes to brainstorm the values that identify you the most. Without referring to any charts or reference material, think about the things that matter to you. Remember your values are those beliefs that are most important to you. Ask yourself the following questions and try to list the things that come to mind. Consider using the notes space for any other thoughts that come to mind.

1. What's important to you?
2. What accomplishments make you feel good about yourself?
3. What values do you call upon in those moments?
4. Think of major decisions you've made. What values did you use to make those choices?
5. What values do you consider a superpower, something you're good at?
6. What values give you strength and give strength to others?

My values are:

_____   _____

_____   _____

_____   _____

_____   _____

_____   _____

_____   _____

Notes

_____

_____

_____

_____

_____

_____

_____

Take a moment and review the values list in the appendix and see if any values resonate with you that you might want to include, or leverage the wording as a better description from what you wrote down. Try to write down your values again by priority. Try to keep the list to no more than five values. Please make a note of why the value is important to you next to it.

Values and Why Important?

_____

_____

_____

_____

_____

_____

_____

_____

YOUR VALUES

You should now have a better sense of what is most important to you and what criteria you use to make your deepest and toughest decisions. Your values list will give you a better sense of self, self-identity, and self-image. There are many values assessments out there should you need more help in defining your values. Do a web search for a free assessment. For a better sense of your values strengths, I recommend www.viacharacter.org, a free assessment that will list your values strengths. We will discuss values strengths in greater detail in the next chapter. You can also contact me at my website www.anthonyperdue.com/purposetopower for more guidance on values awareness.

CHAPTER 8

Self-Awareness Through Strengths

*"Success in the knowledge economy comes to those who know themselves
– their strengths, their values,
and how they best perform"*
——*Peter Drucker*——

Understanding your strengths is another foundational element towards self-awareness, towards clarifying, living, and leading with purpose. A poll conducted by the Gallup organization revealed that only 20% of employees use their work strengths in large corporations. The challenge here is that the poll respondents know what they do not do well but are largely unaware of what they do well.

By now, you may have started to notice the evolutionary pattern that moves from a) an understanding of your story, which b) helps uncover and clarify your values which c) leads to a clear understanding of your strengths. Your story is the foundation of your values, and your values are the foundation of your strengths. Uncovering what you do well is another piece in the puzzle of purpose discovery.

Your strength is a key element to your purpose and your mastery and success in life. The famous organizational management guru, Peter

Drucker, coined the saying, "Success in the knowledge economy comes to those who know themselves – their strengths, values, and how best they perform." Mr. Drucker was well known for many things, including transforming business practices and is widely regarded as the founder of modern management. In 1999 at the ripe young age of 90, Mr. Drucker wrote an article for the Harvard Business Review called *Managing Oneself*. In this article, Mr. Drucker highlighted two areas of specific focus for individuals to manage themselves better. Mr. Drucker felt that the best way to make your greatest contribution and become the best leader and manager you could be was to clearly know your strengths and values. When Mr. Drucker refers to strengths, he encourages understanding job performance strengths, like competency strengths. These strengths focus on our skills, behaviors, talents, and knowledge. Although Mr. Drucker was on to something, not all strengths are related to skills, behaviors, talents, and knowledge competencies.

Values and strengths of values generally focus on two categories - competence or character. The first is competence which has to do with your ability. Strong values of competence can be considered a combination of talent, knowledge, and skills. Talents are formed early in life, from your story, and are further developed through gained knowledge and applied skills. You *value* your talent and further hone it to become a strength through knowledge and application. This competence becomes a strength over time.

The second focus of values is character. Character values focus on elements such as honesty, justice, and mercy. These values align with our virtues, ethics, and morals, which are guideposts in life of good, bad, right, and wrong. Have you ever heard the saying, "do unto others as you would have them do unto you?" This is an example of a character value.

There is a strong correlation between applying your values' strengths in your work and believing that you have found and are walking in your purpose. This leads to the question, "are *you* using your strengths in your work, and are you walking in *your* purpose?" Are you a leader of yourself, utilizing and maximizing your strengths in your purpose?

Strengths-based leadership is the concept and application of having an awareness of your strengths, be they competency, character, or values-based, and intentionally using them on a day to day basis to become a better, stronger, and more effective leader. This means that you can be a better leader of yourself and others by having awareness and maximizing the usage of your strengths in your life and work. The evidence further clarifies that those who turn to and utilize their strengths are in the "top 10% of the organization and can move their perceived leader effectiveness from the bottom 40% to the top 40%."

Perhaps the two most well-known studies of strength of competency and character are from the Gallup organization's Clifton Strengths for competencies and the VIA (values in action) Institute for Character. Both approaches highlight that knowing and utilizing your values strengths lead to a myriad of positive outcomes, from life satisfaction and well-being to finding and knowing your purpose (life meaning). 34 Clifton Strengths highlight four domains of strengths, including strategic thinking, relationship building, influencing, and executing (see table below). Your strengths are a prioritized list of the 34 competencies that are listed below each strength category. The typical measure for Clifton Strengths is to find your 'top five' strengths. For example, my top five are strategic, individualization, relator, learner, and ideation. This means that my main domain of strength is strategic thinking, followed by relationship building. You may look at the list and have an idea where you are strong, but taking the Clifton Strengthsfinder assessment will pinpoint your key strengths.

34 CLIFTON STRENGTHS

Strategic Thinking Analytical, Context, Futuristic, Ideation, Input, Intellection, Learner, Strategic.	**Relationship Building** Adaptability, Connectedness, Developer, Empathy, Harmony, Includer, Individualization, Positivity, Relator
Influencing Activator, Command, Communication, Competition, Maximizer, Self-Assurance, Significance, Woo	**Executing** Achiever, Arranger, Belief, Consistency, Deliberative, Discipline, Focus, Responsibility, Restorative

The VIA Character Strengths assessment operates similarly. It categorizes your key strengths similarly in six domains or themes with 24 character strengths listed within each domain. My top five strengths are creativity, gratitude, love of learning, curiosity, and judgement. The beauty of looking at both is that you will start to notice alignment and overlap between both character and competency strengths across both assessments. I love people (individualization and relator) and seek to learn (learner and curiosity) to come up with ways to help them (strategic, judgment, ideation, and creativity).

24 VIA CHARACTER STRENGTHS

Wisdom Creativity, Curiosity, Judgment, Love of learning, Perspective	**Courage** Bravery, Perseverance, Honesty, Zest	**Humanity** Love, Kindness, Social intelligence
Justice Teamwork, Fairness, Leadership	**Temperance** Forgiveness, Humility, Prudence, Self-regulation	**Transcendence** Appreciation of beauty and excellence, Gratitude, Hope, Humor, Spirituality

You may already be able to look at the list and align your story and values to specific strengths. However, I encourage you to take both assessments in order to clarify your strengths. Feel free to contact me at www.anthonyperdue.com if you would like more guidance with the assessments or clarifying your strengths. I have had coaching clients that were very aware of some strengths while being somewhat surprised and enlightened by others. The exercise below should help get you started on strengths discovery.

STRENGTHS DISCOVERY EXERCISE

The purpose of this exercise is to help you uncover your strengths that will build greater self-awareness and align you to your purpose. Remember that your strengths can be character, virtue, or moral based. Most people have greater clarity of their competencies and skills, but character traits are just as valuable. Refer to both the Strengths Finder list as well as the VIA Character list for inspiration. Ask yourself the following questions:

- What am I the best at doing? Refer to your story for clues.

- What do I do better than 90% of other people?
- What do my coworkers, friends, and family tell me that I am good at doing?
- What are the key activities that you do that make you feel the strongest?
- What do you enjoy doing more than anything on your job?

Make a list of your top 10 strengths

_____

_____

_____

_____

_____

_____

_____

_____

_____

_____

STRENGTHS IN ACTION

Your strengths are your key differentiator to providing value to the world. I recommend that you mull over your list of top 10 strengths and ask yourself the following questions:

- How am I using my strengths on a day-to-day basis?
- How are my strengths changing the world?
- What can I do more of with my strengths that I'm not doing now?
- What impact could I have on the people around me if I used my strengths more?
- How do I feel when I use my strengths?

Using your strengths should make you feel like a superhero. Every superhero has her own unique strengths, and you have yours. Knowledge and utilization of your strengths can make you feel like a million dollars and make others feel equally as special. Let's explore how we can tap into our emotional strengths and the emotions of others in the next chapter.

CHAPTER 9

Self-Awareness Through Emotional Intelligence

"When dealing with people, remember you are not dealing with creatures of logic, but with creatures of emotion."
——*Dale Carnegie*——

Self-awareness is a key skill that will not only serve you in purpose discovery but in life itself—knowing who, what, and why you are is like gaining freedom for the first time in life. It gives us clarity of self which is the key to unlocking so many doors in our lives. Emotional self-awareness is very powerful because it gives us a better understanding of our emotions.

The EQ-i²·⁰® Model

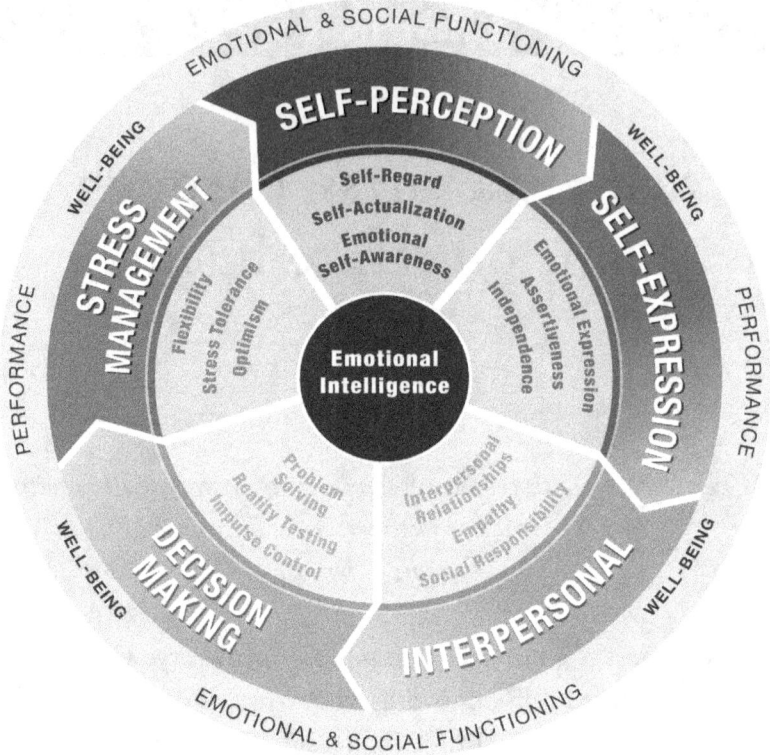

Copyright © 2011 Multi-Health Systems Inc. All rights reserved.
Based on the original BarOn EQ-i authored by Reuven Bar-On, copyright 1997.

There are five main categories of emotional intelligence including a) self-perception, b) self-expression, c) interpersonal, d) decision making, and e) stress management. Each category has three subscales which further clarify that category of emotional intelligence.

EQi Category	Subscale Definitions
Self-Perception	Self-Regard, Self-Actualization, Emotional Self-Awareness
Self-Expression	Emotional Expression, Assertiveness, Independence
Interpersonal	Interpersonal Relationships, Empathy, Social Responsibility
Decision Making	Problem Solving, Reality Testing, Impulse Control
Stress Management	Flexibility, Stress Tolerance, Optimism

Emotional intelligence can go a long way to informing your purpose. First, it can help guide you to greater clarity of your own emotions - emotional self-awareness. Emotional self-awareness is the ability to recognize and understand one's own emotions. It is the ability to understand the subtleties and details of one's emotions and get to those emotions' root cause. Having an awareness of how we feel and why we feel the way we do is a key component of understanding our purpose and having greater self-awareness.

The second reason emotional intelligence can inform our purpose is due to the ability to gain greater clarity of the full spectrum of our emotions, how we use them, how our emotions drive our interactions with others, how we use them to make decisions, and how we handle stress. Having awareness of our emotions and how they manifest in our decisions and actions in life can be a game-changer. Further, not only is there great power in having a recognition of the full spectrum of our emotions but in having recognition of our emotional strengths. For example, if you know that you are very empathetic and are flexible, then perhaps you are more inclined to have a purpose that leans into the skill of listening. If you are a good listener, then that may inform you of a purpose utilizing listening skills. In other words, knowledge of where we are emotionally strong can be key indicators of vocation and purpose. This chapter will explore these two main streams of thought, culminating in translating emotional self-awareness into opportunities to inform your purpose.

EMOTIONAL SELF-AWARENESS FOR PURPOSE DISCOVERY

I'd like you to think about a time that you blew up at someone you cared about, only to end up apologizing later as you reflected on the situation. Most of us have been in a situation where we were angry at someone and lashed out at him even though he was not at fault. Perhaps that lashing out cost you a relationship or friendship. Or perhaps you know someone whose emotional outburst cost them a relationship with you or others. Many of us go our entire lives having emotions that cause us to take them out on others and never deal with them, allowing bitterness, anger, and pain to control our relationships, and in some cases, ultimately our lives. But what if you had the strength to recognize negative emotions in the moment and respond differently? The ability to be emotionally self-aware, especially at the exact time we are feeling certain ways, provides us with the ability and opportunity to change our behavior and actions towards others.

Emotions can also drive our biggest decisions and drive our realization of purpose. Have you ever contemplated your emotions in response to a major life event such as death, tragedy, loss, or even a major win? Could you capture your emotional state that then drove a major decision or action? Some of the greatest people of our time and the past have leveraged emotions, both good and bad, to change the world. What are your world-changing emotions? It is said that emotional self-awareness is the foundation upon which all other elements of emotional intelligence are built. This self-knowledge and self-understanding of emotions can make a major impact on our lives and in the lives of others.

There are four basic emotional families: Anxiety, Anger, Depression, and Contentment. You can most likely recall with ease when you've felt any of these emotions. This is related to emotional self-awareness. Being aware of your emotions helps you recognize them and control them but use them as fuel for purpose discovery and purposeful power. Research and anecdotal evidence show that emotional fuel is largely driven by two main categories: 1) contentment and love, and 2) anger, pain, and fear. Let's explore the two categories and how they can manifest purpose within you.

CONTENTMENT AND LOVE BREEDS PURPOSE

We've all heard, read, and seen love stories that span the history of humankind. One of the most famous love stories is that of Romeo and Juliet. This love-struck tandem was willing to rebuke their feuding families and ultimately die for their love. Love can also be translated into the work of our lives. I have heard people say many times to "do what you love," and the money will come. While I do think there is some truth to that, not everyone is programmed to love a type of work or life's work and dive headfirst into the work at all costs. My son loves to play video games; however, he may find it challenging to earn a living doing what he loves (yes, I know there are video game tournaments that one in 1,000,000 earn a living from).

However, contentment, love, and passion from something can be a major input into your life's purpose. Self-awareness of the contentment you feel from an activity, a cause, or a type of work does indeed exist. The task for you is to find it if that is what motivates you. Take a moment to write down at least ten activities, causes, or work that you love.

10 Things I Love

_____

_____

_____

_____

_____

_____

_____

_____

_____

_____

ANGER, PAIN & FEAR

Anger, pain, and fear are referred to as negative emotions. You, like most people, have deep discomfort for any of the three and most likely try to avoid them at all cost. You can probably think of a time when you were going to try to talk to a man or woman that you liked and got cold feet. That fear of rejection stopped you dead in your tracks. All three emotions can be put to good use in recognition and pursuit of your purpose.

On May 3, 1980, a young girl named Cari Lightner was killed by a driver while driving to a church carnival. It was found that the driver of the vehicle was not only drunk but had multiple infractions for driving under the influence. Cari's mother, Candy Lightner, was so compelled by her daughter's tragic death that she founded the organization Mothers Against Drunk Driving (MADD), which grew into one of the most influential organizations in the country. MADD was formed out of the pain from a tragic event where Candy Lightner was not only distraught from the death of her child but angry that drunk driving laws were not punished harshly.

There may be specific tragedies in your life that have caused you anguish, anger, depression, and pain. Were you able to recognize any of those emotions in your story? If so, how can those events and the associated feelings manifest themselves into a clarification of purpose? Recognizing what makes you angry can be a powerful tool for uncovering your purpose.

On the other hand, although closely related to anger, fear can either drive purpose or hold you back from discovering or even walking in your purpose. In driving purpose, oftentimes, that which we fear is the very thing we care deeply about overcoming. Richard Branson, the CEO of Virgin, strongly believes in George Addair's famous saying, "Everything you've ever wanted is on the other side of fear." In fact, fear can be used as a motivator towards the clarity and realization of your purpose. Dr. Dre, a famous hip-hop producer and rapper, and no, not a real doctor, has a business partner by the name of Jimmy Iovine. Jimmy learned early on to identify his fear and use it as a motivator. In an interview with Complex magazine, Iovine exclaimed that he was propelled to success by "turning fear into a tail wind instead of a head wind." Iovine explains he used his fear to produce the best-engineered music he could, including Bruce Springsteen's classic album, *Born to Run* in 1975. Jimmy used his fear in order to produce some of his best work.

I am generally not a proponent, however, of using negative emotions for positive outcomes. There may be short-term instances where anger, fear, and sadness can drive actions, but the key here is emotional self-awareness and how you choose to use those emotions to become your best self.

In the table below, list what you despise. Perhaps it is something from your story, or perhaps it is something from the present. A word of caution here: I do not want you to force yourself to despise anything. In fact, my preference would be that you would find a source of passion and purpose through something that you love versus something that you despise. However, the reality is that many movements and purpose-driven life's work have come from tragedy and pain. Pain can breed purpose, as you saw from the MADD example earlier.

10 Things I Despise

_____

_____

_____

_____

_____

_____

_____

_____

_____

_____

FEAR: A BLOCKER OF PURPOSE

Let's explore the topic of fear in more detail. While some people like Jimmy Iovine have learned to blast through their fears and harness the energy as a push towards purpose, others have allowed fear to paralyze their dreams. Fear is the one thing that grips so many of us from becoming who we are truly meant to be. Fear grips us all in some way. You can probably think of at least one or two things that scare you. For some, it is the fear of death. For others, it is the fear of something in life (e.g., spiders, snakes, public speaking, etc.).

According to Merriam-Webster, fear is the act of being afraid of something or someone. It can manifest itself in worry and physical, mental, and emotional ways such as sweaty palms, lack of speaking, and lack of action. Fear can become one of the biggest impediments to living a life of purpose. The root cause of fear is our limbic system, which includes the amygdalae organs in our brains. This system detects possibilities for direct pain or even the potential for pain from an unrecognizable event or circumstance. So often times, when we reflect on our purpose and project our purpose in pictures, the vision we see and the person in which we must become can be unrecognizable. When you think about it, the fear of our success in the single most important thing for each of us – being who we were meant to be – sounds not only tragic but unimaginable. Why on earth would we be afraid of becoming the best version of ourselves?

According to the research, fear is rooted in the history of humankind's harmful events and our brains' development throughout this history and our own lived experiences caused by painful confrontations, loss of loved ones, loss of social status, rejection, and physical injury. So in some instances, the actual projection of ourselves into an unknown place can cause an amygdalae response, triggering emotions of fear, worry, and anxiety.

The good news is that fear can be dealt with through self-awareness and an acceptance of the fear. Ironically, being both aware of the fear or the negative emotion and fully accepting it as a reality is the beginning of your freedom from it. Just like Jimmy Iovine, if you can gain awareness of your fear, you can push through the fear and overcome it. Here are some tips for identifying and overcoming fear if this applies to you:

1. **Perceive Your Fear** – According to a Columbia University study, when fear is perceived consciously, the brain itself can tamp down amygdalae activity. So, write it down. Write down what is making

you afraid and fully perceive it. Do not run away from it, rather name the fear in real terms.
2. **Accept the Fear** – One of the keys to overcoming fear is to accept that it exists and that you are indeed afraid. Once you perceive the fear, choose to accept that you are afraid.
3. **Evaluate and Decide** – Once you can perceive and accept the fear, you can calmly determine whether you will do something about it, avoid it, or live with it. When you can quiet the fear through perception and acceptance, your rational mind can calmly decide what to do about it. You can choose to confidently decide to 'face your fear' or avoid it altogether.
4. **Meditation and Mindfulness** - Meditation can also help build emotional self-awareness. Taking the time to relax and focus your mind can reveal emotions that we may not easily see within ourselves unless we slow down and become present. There are several meditation and mindfulness apps, videos, and audio sources to consider.
5. **Express Gratitude** – Gratitude has been scientifically proven to improve your emotional state and relieve anxiety. Make a list of at least three things that you are grateful for daily.
6. **Turn Off the Source** – Today's world is full of many fear triggers, including pandemics, economic despair, political unrest, environmental challenges, and the like. While it can help to stay up on certain current events, too much bad news consumption can keep us in a state of fear. Do like my mom used to tell me and "turn off the TV!"

LAYING YOUR PURPOSE FOUNDATION WITH EMOTIONAL INTELLIGENCE

We have explored emotional self-awareness and how those emotions can be used to drive purpose. The overcoming of fear is also important in the realization of your purpose. Emotional self-awareness can be used to awaken the purpose within you. The recognition of your emotions can be used to identify what you care deeply about and which you can do something about. Follow the steps below to clarify your emotional self-awareness and identify potential pathways to your purpose discovery.

Step One – Identify What You Love or Despise

I would like you to take the top five things in either category and write them down below in the left-most column. Think about the MADD example above.

Step Two – Identify Your Emotions

I would like you to continue with the exercise by reflecting on how the things you either love or despise makes you feel. What are your emotions in response to what you love or despise?

Step Three – What Can You Do About It

In the corresponding third column, I'd like you to also reflect on what you can do about what you love and/or despise. In the MADD example, the mother of a daughter killed in a drunk driving accident started an organization that sparked a movement across the United States. Is there something that you love or despise and makes you feel strongly enough to start a movement, a business, or a social enterprise?

I Love / Despise	Makes Me Feel	What Can I Do About it?
e.g., I love dogs and despise when they are treated badly.	e.g., It makes me sad beyond belief to know that a puppy is mistreated.	e.g., I can start an awareness campaign to ensure puppies are treated better. I can provide owner education to owning a happy puppy and pet.

We will revisit these elements in the next chapter. But first, I'd like to go deeper in the understanding of the full spectrum of emotions and how the strengths of emotions can also be used to propel you into a life of purpose.

EMOTIONAL INTELLIGENCE STRENGTHS

My daughter Juliah often refers to herself as 'quarter dog.' Now I know this might seem beyond strange, but it is actually a self-identified and highly observable gift that she has. She often lets out the sound "aww" when she sees a cute animal. In fact, at the age of ten, she exclaimed, "I can talk to animals, and therefore, I am no longer eating them." She became a pescatarian and has been so for the past three years. Juliah has emotional strengths of empathy, emotional expression, and social responsibility.

As mentioned earlier in the chapter, Multi-Health Systems (MHS) refers to 15 subscales of emotional intelligence in their Emotional Intelligence 2.0 (EQ-I 2.0) model. Research shows that top performers in their respective fields of law, leadership, entrepreneurship, finance, medicine, sales, and so on share certain emotional intelligence subscales' strengths. For example, lawyers tend to score higher in Independence, Optimism, Reality Testing, and Stress Tolerance. You can see from the basic definitions here that a good lawyer would need to a) work independently, b) express optimism for themselves and their clients, c) have a strong sense of logic, reality, and logical thought, and d) be able to handle an enormous amount of stress, depending on the type of law practiced and caseload.

The alignment of our emotional strengths with our purpose and life's work reveals two things. First, it gives us a sense of what profession or work will be a natural fit. In my daughter's case, she has already expressed a strong interest in becoming a veterinarian and helping animals in some great capacity. The good news is that her emotional strengths are already aligned to that potential life's work.

The second reason alignment of our emotional strengths with our purpose is important is how it makes us feel. Studies in positive psychology show that the more we can utilize our strengths, the higher our well-being and engagement. In other words, we are most happy when our emotional strengths align with our purpose. It is for this reason that an understanding of your emotional strengths can strongly inform your purpose.

Below you will find two approaches to informing purpose through emotional intelligence strengths. The table below offers up a general alignment of emotional strengths to specific career types. The research conducted generally supports the emotional intelligence elements that are the strongest for the top performers in that respective field.

Profession	Emotional Intelligence Strengths
Entrepreneurs	Empathy, Interpersonal Relationships, Social Responsibility, Flexibility, Stress Tolerance, and Optimism
Educators	Self-Actualization, Problem Solving, Optimism, Stress Tolerance, and Happiness
Sales	Interpersonal Relationships, Self-Actualization, Empathy, Flexibility, and Stress Tolerance
Law Enforcement	Social Responsibility, Problem Solving, Self-Actualization, and Interpersonal Relationships

Purpose can be informed through emotional intelligence by understanding how your sub-scale strengths align to general competency areas. Competencies such as listening, compassion, problem-solving, patience, and being action-oriented can all indicate an alignment towards purpose. The table below shows how certain emotional intelligence elements align with these competencies.

Workplace Competency	Aligned EQ-I Element
Action Oriented	Self-Regard, Self-Actualization, Optimism, Independence
Approachability	Interpersonal Relationships, Impulse Control, Flexibility
Caring About Direct Reports	Interpersonal Relationships, Social Responsibility, Empathy
Compassion	Compassion Interpersonal Relationships, Empathy
Composure	Impulse Control, Reality Testing, Emotional Self-Awareness, Stress
Conflict Management	Problem Solving, Interpersonal Relationships, Empathy, Independence,
Customer Focus	Interpersonal Relationships, Empathy, Problem Solving, Social
Decision Quality	Independence, Reality Testing, Problem Solving, Impulse Control
Interpersonal Savvy	Interpersonal Relationships, Empathy
Listening	Empathy, Flexibility
Managerial Courage	Self-Regard, Self-Actualization, Optimism, Independence, Reality Testing
Organizational Agility	Self-Regard, Self-Actualization, Optimism, Flexibility
Patience	Impulse Control, Stress Tolerance, Flexibility

Peer Relationships	Interpersonal Relationships, Empathy
Perseverance	Self-Regard, Self-Actualization, Optimism, Stress Tolerance, Flexibility
Personal Disclosure	Emotional Expression, Assertiveness, Interpersonal Relationships
Self-Knowledge	Emotional Self-Awareness, Reality Testing
Standing Alone	Independence, Assertiveness, Self-Regard, Self-Actualization, Optimism

WHAT ARE YOUR EMOTIONAL INTELLIGENCE STRENGTHS?

The best way to uncover your emotional strengths is to take an assessment from a well-known and scientifically backed EQ assessment instrument. I am most familiar with the EQi-2.0 model from MHS, but there are also others out there. To get a better sense of your emotional intelligence, go to my website and contact me for the assessment. I am certified in the EQi-2.0 assessment tool and can help you better understand your emotional intelligence strengths.

There are other online tools for uncovering your emotional intelligence strengths as well. Whether you take the MHS EQi-2.0 assessment or another assessment, I suggest you list your top five emotional strengths and reflect on how those strengths can contribute to your life's work. In the next section, you will rank your EQ strengths in the column on the right—the corresponding columns on the left list what potential purposeful activity would align well to this strength. You should notice one of two phenomena. The first is that you will recall elements from your story and your self-awareness. You should start to see alignment between key elements of your story, your values, your emotions of things you love and despise, as well as your emotional intelligence strengths.

If you are not ready to dive in and take an assessment, the other way to get a sense of your emotional intelligence strengths is to write down what you think they are and test them against how others see you. Remember objective self-awareness from a previous chapter? The best way to ensure that you see yourself in the correct light is to test objectivity against how others see you. It may be a bit of a challenge to get to the level of specificity of emotional strengths that an assessment would afford. However, you can at least start to get a sense of how others see you and see your emotional strengths. For instance, someone might see you as a good listener and very empathetic. Perhaps you have a social cause in the world that you care deeply about, like sustainability or clean energy. Feedback can assist you in better understanding your emotional strengths.

YOUR EMOTIONAL INTELLIGENCE STRENGTHS EXERCISE

In this exercise, you will develop a list of your top five emotional strengths. Walk through the steps below to try to get as much clarity as possible on your emotional strengths. Please keep in mind that this exercise will help you clarify your emotional strengths but is not as effective as an in-depth EQ assessment. However, it is a good place to start if you are not ready to take an assessment.

Step One – EQ Strength Ranking

Start by reflecting on the strengths in the table below. For each strength statement, decide whether or not you believe you are strong in that area by answering yes or no (Y/N).

EQ Strengths	EQ Category	Y/N
I always feel good about myself	Self-Regard	
I am clear on my life's purpose	Self-Actualization	
I am always aware of how I feel	Emotional Self-Awareness	
I easily express myself	Emotional Expression	
I am highly assertive	Assertiveness	
I make my best decisions by myself	Independence	
I am a great friend	Interpersonal Relationships	
I am a great listener	Empathy	
I feel strongly about social issues	Social Responsibility	
I love to solve problems	Problem Solving	
I easily see things for what they are	Reality Testing	
I always weigh options before action	Impulse Control	
I am highly adaptable to new things	Flexibility	
I handle stress very well	Stress Tolerance	
I always see the glass half full	Optimism	

Step Two – Do They Agree?

Once you have completed step one above, you are now ready to test your self-awareness with those who know you best. Try to select at least three people to review your list with and see what feedback you get. Do they agree or disagree with your self-assessment? Ask them the following two questions:

1. What do you think my top five emotional strengths are and why?
2. Where do you agree or disagree the most with my assessment?

Step Three – Top Five Emotional Intelligence Strengths

After you have shared your list with at least three people and gained feedback, reflect on the insight you gained and create your top five list below. List the EQ strengths on the left and why you believe that is your strength on the right. Your why can come from your story, self-awareness examples, or feedback from others. It is important to list your why to clarify the reason behind your belief and strengthen the belief itself.

_____

_____

_____

_____

_____

Understanding your emotional self-awareness and your EQ strengths is key to being self-aware and gaining clarity of purpose. The list that you created above should serve as a foundational element for gaining greater self-awareness. Understanding the full spectrum of your emotional strengths will allow you to clarify a major pillar of self-awareness which is a key to unlock the door of purpose.

CHAPTER 10

Self-Awareness Summary

"Look outside, and you will see yourself. Look inside, and you will find yourself."
——*Drew Gerald*——

Congratulations! If you've read this far through this book, you should be congratulated and very proud of yourself. Doing the work to create better self-awareness is one of the most difficult things you can do in self-development and leadership. In all of my leadership training and coaching sessions, the most difficult challenge is the challenge of self-discovery. I have seen many instances of mid to high-level managers and leaders take the focus off of themselves and shift to their teams. Self-awareness takes courage. The process of building self-awareness takes an ability to get to know and accept your "as-is" version.

You have not only embarked on the journey of building self-awareness but have completed a major milestone. You have explored your values, your strengths, and your deepest emotions. The combination of these three pillars should give you a better sense of who you are. With your values, you have a better sense of your beliefs, what you hold dear, what is important to you, and the basis on which you make the most important decisions in your life.

driven by my values of _____

_____ which

make me feel _____

and I can use my key strengths of (competency strengths and

emotional strengths) _____

_____ in order to

make the following changes in the world _____

_____

_____

    The combination of your beliefs, values, emotions, and strengths can have an enormous impact on what you see in the world that needs to change. This change can be as simple as ensuring everyone in your neighborhood picks up their trash to ridding the world of nuclear weapons. This change can be expressed through service, like the bridge between thinking about your purpose and becoming your purpose. In the next chapter, we will explore how to put the changes you want to make in the world to work through service.

CHAPTER 11

Purpose Through Serving Others

"Service to others is the rent you pay for your room here on earth."
——*Muhammad Ali*——

In 2016, I was a part of a massive layoff of the IBM Corporation. I found myself in an unfamiliar territory of job loss. I worked at the company for 18 years, a part of an exclusive executive leadership group, and found myself in a state of disbelief. What I didn't know at the time was that the job loss was actually a blessing for me, and the swift kick in the you know what strengthened my journey in my purpose and to serve others.

One of the first things I realized about losing my job is that it presented me with an opportunity to hit the reset button in my career and thrust me into my life's purpose. It was an opportunity for me to shift from a job that was not aligned with my life's purpose towards a career and life's work that were much more meaningful and aligned with my purpose. This event presented an opportunity for me to take the time to self-reflect and gain more clarity on who I was and who I wanted to become in my life and my work. It also allowed me to clarify my purpose and the vision of my purpose that I wanted to see come to fruition.

About a month after my layoff, I began volunteering as a leadership trainer and coach at a workforce development program in inner-city Baltimore. Volunteering was one of the most magical and gratifying experiences of my life. Volunteering allowed me to utilize my gifts and competencies in my purpose and gave me fulfillment and meaning in life that I never experienced while working at my previous corporation. It is difficult to put into words how helping your fellow brothers or sisters create a better existence for themselves and their families makes you feel. It made me feel grateful. It allowed me to experience so much gratitude that the fear and doubts that I had from job loss had little to no room to exist or operate within me.

Serving gave my work meaning and allowed me to help others who had situations far more challenging than my own. It was as though I experienced another level of gratitude, "super-gratitude," and it can be experienced when serving others in your purpose. The key here is to get to a place where you can align with your purpose, passions, and strengths. This is why knowing your story and having a full understanding of values, beliefs, emotions, and strengths is so important to being in service to others.

SERVICE: THE PATH TO PURPOSE

Prior to my layoff, I had already begun the journey of seeking and actualizing my life's purpose. As I have previously mentioned, I knew that my purpose was to help others to find their purpose and be the best leaders of themselves, their families, their businesses, and their communities. While knowing this statement, an expression of my purpose, was a good thing in my mind, it didn't easily translate to knowing what to do.

For me, I decided to get educated. In 2011 I began reading as many books on leadership as I could. I also interviewed leaders and teachers. The leaders I interviewed gave me insights into their intentional behaviors that allowed them to influence others. The leadership teachers gave me insights into how they developed into their work and some keys for being effective. With all of this insight, I decided to return to school to pursue a Doctor of Strategic Leadership (DSL). So, while I worked my day job at IBM, I attended school at night to further the journey towards my destiny.

There is a strong lesson here in charting your path to your purpose. Most of us don't have the luxury of abruptly switching careers or your life's work if you work in a job that requires, at a minimum, 40 hours of your time every week. The lesson here is that you must work after your work. Walking in your purpose will require sacrifice! But the sacrifice will more than be worth it.

Christopher Taylor, the founder of the Occupation Optimist and expert on career and job hunt strategies, found his purpose in helping people to find jobs through recruiting services. The challenge for Chris was that he had never been a recruiter and had a background in sales. Chris began volunteering for Friends of Refugees, an organization that helps refugees find work. Through service, he was able to gain experience in job recruiting while doing meaningful work in his purpose. Chris reported that not only did he find joy in his work, but that it actually reduced his stress and anxiety, helped to build his network, and ultimately enabled his career transition in alignment with his purpose.

PATH TO PURPOSE EXERCISE

The statement of self-awareness that I had you write in the last chapter should help you get closer to clarifying your purpose, but it may still seem cloudy. I am hopeful that you will have at least been able to identify, on some level, your values and beliefs, your strengths, and what makes you feel joy and happiness, and what makes you mad, fearful, or anxious. Between your story and your growing self-awareness, you should be able to identify at least two to three "target areas" of where you would like to focus your energy. This energy can be in the form of changing the world or just picking up trash in the local park.

Only you know what that focus could and should be. Write down those changes in the space below. You might have a focus on one specific change, or there may be many. List those things which might be as specific as 10% cleaner air and eradicate child poverty in my city, or as general as reducing homelessness or giving more opportunities to families for homeownership. There are countless ways that you can help change the world based upon what really motivates you and what you are good at. Try to be as exhaustive and explicit as possible.

_____

_____

_____

_____

_____

_____

_____

_____

Now take a look at what you wrote, the change that you want to see happen. If you are currently in a position where you already have an impact on making the change happen that you want to see, then that's a great place to be. If you cannot make change happen, ask yourself what you could be doing to contribute to making the change that you want to see. Perhaps you already have a for-profit or non-profit business that you need to restart or blow the dust off the business plan. Or perhaps you have an opportunity at your place of work to do some additional work with a community team or start a volunteer effort with a group of like-minded coworkers.

Remember you don't have to do everything by yourself. In fact, the change that you want to make is most likely too small if you can manage it all by yourself. On a scale that has a great impact, service to the world will require a team, partnerships, and collaboration. In fact, teaming with someone in service to others can be the main driver towards fulfilling your purpose. In the timeless book, *Think and Grow Rich*, Napoleon Hill explains how a gentleman named Edwin C. Barnes had a definite purpose and burning desire to work alongside Thomas A. Edison and become his business partner. He did not know Mr. Edison at all, but with desire, persistence, and determination, he became Mr. Edison's business partner and helped drive the Edison Dictating Machine's mass adoption. So if you have a motivation for service in an area that others may have more experience or more reach, you should strongly consider a partnership in your volunteerism or service.

Whether it's a partnership or just the volunteering of your time, I'd like you to think about any specific people or organizations that are seeking the same or a similar change as you. Write those names and/or organizations in the space below. If you are unclear of any specific people or organizations, I suggest you do a bit of research to find out the top five organizations in your area that are working in the same area of your interest. You could also tap into your personal or social network as well with the question, "does anyone know who is involved in *this* type of service work?"

Potential Volunteer Opportunities:

_____

_____

_____

_____

_____

_____

_____

_____

_____

SERVE INTO PURPOSE

To this point, you may be telling yourself, "all this is good stuff, but I still have no idea what my purpose is. Not only that, I'm not even 100% sure what it is I want to change, or even what I want to volunteer in." If that is you, that's okay. I encourage continuous soul searching to gain clarity and conviction on identifying what you care about; but no, you are not a lost cause. But I'd like you to consider another approach to purpose discovery if you are still unsure. Think about a scale from 1 – 10 with a ten score representing a score of great clarity of purpose. This ten score represents the same clarity of purpose that an 8K TV represents - high-definition clarity. I hope that everyone who reads this book and follows through on the plan develops their clarity of purpose to a ten score. I truly hope that at this point, you don't have a score of one – absolutely no clue or direction of purpose.

If I were to guess, I would imagine that most of you are somewhere in the middle. You have a deeper understanding of your story, your self-awareness, and a sense of what you care enough about to give of your time. There may even be two or three areas or "target zones" that are top of mind. That said, I know that it is unrealistic for everyone to have clarity of purpose just from reading one book or getting through a few exercises. Perhaps you have a sense of the type of people you want to help, a cause you want to fight for, or a societal problem that you want to help solve or contribute to addressing in some way.

Whether you have clarity of purpose and service or are unclear – volunteer, I suggest that you just go and volunteer regardless of where you are in your clarity of purpose. Why do I say this, you might ask? I say this because just volunteering can help you find purpose just in the act of service. In other words, you can back into the feeling of purpose from serving someone or something else that is meaningful to that person or to that cause. Take cancer patient and survivor Roxie Loudenslager, for example. When talking to a news reporter about what gave her the drive to continue to fight her cancer, Roxie exclaimed, "every day is important because there is always something to do. Volunteer opportunities give me purpose." Roxie simply made sandwiches for her local church on Saturdays to distribute to residents in need. The act of her service and volunteer efforts gave her purpose.

This same effect showed up even more with Tillie O'Neal-Kyles, who started volunteering after retirement as a telecommunications executive. Mrs. O'Neal-Kyles searched for volunteer opportunities and decided to help other women, like herself, a single mom, who had a tough time financially, despite having a career that she could be proud of. That desire to help led her to volunteering at the Mary Hall Freedom House, an Atlanta-based nonprofit that provides health and counseling services, along with transitional housing to women and children.

While Mrs. O'Neal-Kyles found fulfillment in her volunteer efforts, a fire was lit inside her to do more. She had discovered her purpose in the service and decided to expand upon this halfway-house model. While appreciative of the opportunity to volunteer, she recognized some gaps in delivering services to women that she decided to close. She founded a comprehensive program called Every Woman Works, which has helped over 2100 women get back on their feet through an eight-week, boot-camp style, coaching, and job training program. Mrs. O'Neal-Kyles found her purpose through service later in life. At 75, she recognized how her purpose gave her life, stating, "I see some of my retired friends who are sick, and I think it's because they have no purpose in life... You've got to continue to be useful to the world, or you just wither away."

SERVICE & PURPOSE – BENEFITS OF A TWO-WAY STREET

The lesson here is that purpose can be expressed through service, and service can drive purpose. It is a two-way street. The traffic can flow one way or the other, or even both ways at one time. The act of service can drive feelings of purpose and greater clarity of purpose itself. The clarity and knowledge of your purpose, or at least knowledge of a general direction of your purpose target areas, can aim and direct your volunteer and service efforts.

Both starting points are powerful. They work hand in hand to create a symbiotic relationship, where the energy, focus, and effort put into one, greatly enhances and benefits the other. The greater clarity of purpose, the greater focus and impact you can have in service. The greater your efforts of service, the greater your feelings of purpose. There are three main benefits of this relationship that are realized when the work begins: 1) feelings of significance, 2) driving and receiving value, and 3) connecting to a higher calling.

I wrote earlier in this chapter about how I experienced so many benefits of serving others after my layoff. I mentioned how I felt so grateful to the point of experiencing "super gratitude." I also felt a strong significance to the work I was doing. I remember as a salesman, trying to convince myself that I was making a difference in the world by helping to drive the adoption of cell phones and help with customer service efforts at major wireless telecommunications companies. Yes, I could connect the dots with how I was making an impact, but it was always a stretch in my thoughts to connect to significance. Significance comes when we feel as though we are making an impact on something that really matters. Cell phones are nice to have items. Food, shelter, and clothing are necessities. When I volunteered to help people develop life and workplace skills to feed their families, that's when I felt significance. I felt that I was making a difference in people's lives that could determine their survival and their families' ability to escape the vicious cycles of poverty in the Baltimore area.

The second benefit of serving in purpose is the value that you give and receive. Yes, the more you give unto others, the greater potential there is to receive. And yes, this does include monetary value. The volunteer work that Christopher Taylor started with Friends of Refugees resulted in his ability to gain relevant experience in his purpose. This volunteering led to his starting his business and gaining new clients. In other words, Chris received from the value he gave. His volunteer efforts in his purpose have paid off in many ways, including monetarily.

Lastly, serving others in purpose has the benefit of granting us proximity with a higher calling. Many world religions and spiritual movements share the ideal that there is a higher power and that we as human beings seek a connection with that power. Serving in purpose can give us a feeling of being connected to our higher selves, a higher calling, and those who believe – our God and creator. Purposeful service can be a pull towards a meaningful mission, a mission that has been placed inside of you to find. A mission that has been discovered by you to be acted upon through service to your fellow woman or man. A mission that God has purposed. Not only can you derive the benefits of service directly, the clarification of purpose and the service you give describe the impact that you will have on planet earth, in eternal space and time. It is your gift given to the world that so shines before men and women, as a star shines unto the universe.

CHAPTER 12

The Realization and Clarity of Purpose

"Through the triumphs there has come a greater confidence and through the challenges has come a greater clarity of purpose."
——O. J. Briganc——

If you've made it this far in the book, I commend you. The act of pursuing more clarity of your purpose so that you can unleash an unparalleled power in your life puts you in rare company. Those who know they are born for a purpose and seek to realize it are rare breeds. The other thing to acknowledge is that the process of realizing your purpose is often fraught with some of the most challenging times of your life. I fully recognize that my purpose was born out of pain experienced over many years of fatherlessness, homelessness, and aimlessness.

Some of you may be in the midst of a challenging time, and the clarification and realization of your purpose are not coming to you as fast as you'd like. To you, I say, don't give up. You will find your purpose, and it will bring you change, energy, and power in your life.

At the age of 17, DC native Chris Wilson was tried as an adult and sentenced to life in prison for murder. By that time, five of his friends had been murdered, along with his father. It is incomprehensible to most people that someone sentenced to life in prison could believe that he has a purpose and could change his circumstances.

But that's exactly what Chris Wilson did. After a year in prison, Chris was determined that he would live a life of purpose. He was determined to turn his life around, build a business, and eventually teach other returning citizens to do the same. He was eventually released from prison after 16 years and not only put his purpose into action but has become one of the most influential people in the City of Baltimore and has employed hundreds of people. Chris has visited the White House twice and has been recognized by many media outlets for his accomplishments.

I share Chris's story to show you that purpose can give you power no matter who you are, what you've done, or what your current circumstances are. Purpose can be clarified and realized by anyone.

GAINING CLARITY OF PURPOSE

The previous chapters on gaining clarity of purpose focused on a set of three main elements – your story, your self-awareness, and your service to others and the world. The combination of those three areas of focus gives us clarity of purpose. Your story culminates your past self, your life milestones, themes, accomplishments, and your setbacks. Self-awareness is the great foundation for clarifying who you are, your deepest beliefs and values, strengths, and character. Service gives you clarity of where to aim the arrow of your story and the best of who you are, guiding it to its destination for divine impact on the world.

Story + Self-Awareness + Service=Purpose

Now it's time for the rubber to meet the road. It is time to clarify your purpose in words that describe who you are through your story elements, self-awareness, and service to others. On the next page, I would like you to complete the purpose summary areas to begin to culminate the elements of your purpose together in a cohesive way.

LIFE PURPOSE SUMMARY

I want you to write down the main thoughts and themes of your purpose in the categories below. You should have some or most of the elements from the exercises in the previous chapters. Here we start to materialize your purpose together from the elements.

STORY THEMES

The first elements I'd like you to focus on are your story themes. In a previous chapter, I had you do the Bourne Identity exercise. Each time frame in your life should have produced a theme aligned with something you learned about yourself or about life. If you recall, these stories and themes helped to define who you are, your beliefs, values, and passions. Write down the top theme that comes to mind. What area or areas of your life stand out the most? Specifically, what do you care most deeply about as a result of your story? Think back to the passion, pain, and promotion elements of story development. You should be able to identify at least one or two things that you care deeply about.

In the space below, write down what you care about the most from those themes that stand out.

_____

_____

_____

_____

_____

SELF-AWARENESS

Write down your core values

Write down your strengths

_____

_____

_____

_____

_____

_____

_____

Write down your emotional self-awareness. This can be driven by the story themes and what you care most deeply about. In other words, how does what you care about make you feel? Also, look to the outcome of your EQ-I assessments or self-evaluation.

_____

_____

_____

_____

_____

_____

_____

_____

_____

_____

Write who you can serve and how, leveraging what you care about most, how your values and strengths can be of good use to whom you can serve and how, and how you would feel when you served others in that capacity.

_____

_____

_____

_____

_____

_____

_____

_____

LIFE PURPOSE STATEMENT

The life purpose statement begins to create a one-sentence understanding of who you are and what you are born to do. The life purpose statement is *your* source of ultimate power. It is your purpose and the fuel that burns the fire of your life.

There are essentially three elements to the life purpose statement – why, what, and how. We begin with why to highlight the significance and importance of your purpose to the world. The 'why' typically starts with the word 'to' in order to state from the beginning why you are here. The why also usually focuses on the service and value that you are meant to give to others. Check out the examples below.

- To improve the lives of people and families
- To teach others
- To eradicate poverty
- To serve as a leader
- To end racism
- To end child abuse

The second element describes what you will do to address the 'why' that has been identified. You will identify the service you will provide to the world. Here, your life experiences and the core elements of who you are reflected in service to mankind. The 'what' part of the purpose statement can start with anything you would like, but the words 'in order to' can help clarify what you seek to do. Here are some examples below:

- In order to help men to become better fathers
- In order to help returning citizens
- In order to cultivate the self-worth and net-worth of women

- In order to bring awareness to better education

The last element of your purpose statement is optional as it goes into some level of detail of how you will use your gifts. It can focus on your values and strengths that you will utilize to be of service. It is a reminder, and an affirmation to you, of the tools you possess that have been bestowed upon you to best serve others. As an aside, if you see others' mission or purpose statements, you may not see this part added, generally because people don't see it as a valuable part of the statement. I think it is important to remind ourselves of our uniqueness and the affirmation of those unique elements. You may choose to begin adding this part of the purpose statement and removing it later. Here are examples of the 'how' below:

- By utilizing my creativity, curiosity, spirituality, ability to relate to others, and strategic thinking
- Using my gifts of empathy and caring for others
- Leveraging my passion for caring for animals
- Using my strengths of communication and artistic abilities

Now, let's put that all together and see what it looks like. I'll start with my own purpose statement. My purpose is as follows:

> *To improve the lives of families, businesses, and communities by developing them to be purposeful leaders, utilizing my gifts of creativity, strategic thinking, problem-solving, and relationship building.*

Now, why don't you give it a try? Remember, this is a journey and something that will evolve over time. For some, the purpose statement comes easy and will forever be written in stone. For others, it takes time for the statement to sink in and grow roots of truth and belief. Write down your purpose statement to the best of your ability below.

Purpose Statement

_____

_____

_____

_____

_____

_____

_____

_____

REFLECTION

This is the part of the journey where I would like you to reflect on your true purpose. Read your purpose statement out loud. Share your purpose statement with others and have discussions around its significance. My hope for you is that you see your purpose statement much like you would see a newborn laying in a crib or basket full of life and a promising future. I encourage you to write and rewrite your statement in bold letters, in calligraphy, on a white board, in 48-font, printed out, or posted on your wall.

The point here is that this should be a moment to celebrate if you have gained clarity for your life purpose. You must recognize this as both a milestone and a moment of significance towards your future. The true meaning of life is to find its meaning, its purpose, so that you can live a life in the fullness that it was meant to be lived.

Purpose goes beyond just understanding yourself. It is a pull towards a meaningful mission and describes the impact you will have on planet earth in eternal space and time. It is your gift given to the world that so shines before men and women as a star unto the universe. As with all bright lights, it must expand outward to cover a multitude of people. You must also expand outward from your purpose as the inception of light, but not as the complete end state. The work must continue, the purpose must come to life in order to experience power.

PART THREE

How to Walk in Your Purpose

CHAPTER 13

Purpose in Pictures – Creating Your Vision

"Vision is the art of seeing what is invisible to others."
——*Jonathan Swift*——

You most likely have a clearer sense of your purpose at this point than you did when you first picked up the book. The good news is that you solved the most difficult part of the process in fulfilling your full potential and full power. However, the work is not done. To experience full power and fulfill your potential, your purpose must become a manifestation of reality. This manifestation is likened to a planted seed that requires other elements to mature into a full-grown tree and eventually produce fruit. Your purpose is like this seed. Your purpose, just like the seed, contains the DNA, the critical information that informs what will come to life. While purpose is the critical element, it cannot grow into a full life by itself. Like the seed, your purpose must be planted in good soil, fertilized, exposed to light and water, and given time and attention to fully express itself through visible evidence of life.

The other elements that allow a purpose to grow into life include vision, strategy, planning, and execution. Purpose drives vision, vision drives strategy and planning, and once you have the map and road to your destination, it will allow you to execute with maximum effectiveness and efficiency to make things happen to fulfill your purpose. This chapter focuses on the establishment of your vision and strategic plan.

VISION

In the Netflix show *Ozark*, Marty Byrde, the lead character who just so happens to be a money launderer living in the Midwest for a Mexican drug cartel, gets thrown into an underground prison. His captor, the drug cartel head Omar Navarro, asks him one simple question, "what do you want?" The two men go back and forth for days with Marty crying, yelling, and pleading for his life. Finally, Marty begins to bring his intense truth to the surface, telling Navarro that he hopes that they chop his head off. Navarro calmly says, "That's a start." Marty does go on to clarify exactly what he wants, laundering money only when 'he' thinks it's safe. Now I certainly don't condone Marty's chosen profession, but I use this example to illustrate that there may be a moment, a pit-like moment, where we have to wrestle with ourselves as to what we truly want and desire.

Your ultimate intrinsic desire, driven by your purpose, is the cornerstone of power. It is the fuel, the vehicle, and the destination to your greatness. Napoleon Hill describes this desire this way, stating, "there is one quality which one must possess to win, and that is the definiteness of purpose, the knowledge of what one wants, and a burning desire to possess it." This desire inspires when, not if, you are met with failure. Mr. Hill further writes of Thomas Edison and how he "dreamed of a lamp that could be operated by electricity... to put his dream into action, and *despite more than 10,000 failures*, he stood by that dream until he made it a physical reality. Practical dreamers do not quit!"

Mr. Edison, just like Marty Byrde, ultimately figured out exactly what he wanted and persevered after failing 10,000 times! Mr. Edison's purpose was to maniacally invent solutions that the world needed. His vision was to create inventions that were commercially viable to the masses, including the incandescent light bulb. Realizing what you want is different from realizing why you want it. Purpose is the intrinsic knowledge of why you are who you are. Vision is the understanding of how that purpose will manifest itself into a specified reality. Purpose is the tip of an arrow pointed in the direction towards your destiny and towards the fulfillment of becoming the best version of yourself. Becoming the best version of yourself, however, takes knowing what that will actually look like. This manifestation is called vision. Vision is the long-term or ultimate outcome we want to see materialize from what we care deeply about the most. In other words, vision is our purpose in pictures. With vision, we can literally *see* our future. Vision is purpose painted on a wall or canvas for all to see.

Vision and purpose go hand in hand and are a yin and yang, equal elements of a powerful energy source, direction, and life itself. Peter M. Senge, the great management consultant and author of the book, *The Fifth Discipline, The Art & Practice of the Learning Organization*, describes the relationship between purpose and vision this way:

> *Real vision cannot be understood in isolation from the idea of purpose. By purpose, I mean an individual's sense of why he or she is alive. No one could prove or disprove the statement that human beings have purpose, but vision is different from purpose. Purpose is similar to a direction, a general heading. Vision is a specific destination, a picture of the desired future. Purpose is advancing man's capability to explore the heavens. Vision is a man on the Moon by the end of the 1960s. Purpose is being the best I can be, excellence. Vision is breaking the four-minute mile.*

Mr. Senge's description and the relationship between vision and purpose should clarify that although purpose and vision are different, they are aligned in their importance independently and with one another towards growth in all aspects of humankind. The relationship between the two is inextricably linked and interdependent, like a wife and husband, the earth and the moon, and food and water.

MAKE THE TARGET CLEAR

One of the funniest moments that I have had with my children is laughing at my vision board. A vision board consists of pictures, magazine clippings, words, and just about anything you can visualize that describes your vision on a poster-sized board. I created this vision board to consistently remind myself of what I wanted in life and what it will look like in the future. My kids were laughing at a picture of my face on someone's body with six-pack abdominals and less than 10% body fat. While embarrassing to reflect upon and even more so to write, it has given me a target to try to achieve. While I'm not quite there, I am at least clear where I want to go physically. However, the book you are reading now is one part of my vision board that has manifested itself into a reality.

I have set a long-term vision for myself as a leadership development trainer, coach, author, and speaker. I have a vision for what I ultimately want and goals and milestones along the path. I encourage you to make your target clear and to articulate your vision, goals, and milestones towards walking in your purpose.

One of the key exercises to help you clarify your vision is to write a news story, magazine article, or blog about your life. Think about how it would be for the top news and information outlets in the country and even the world to write an expose on your life. What would they say about you? How would they describe the impact you made in your family, your community, in your business dealings, and in the world? Would they write about your purpose and your character? Would they write about key moments in your life of high achievement and high impact?

Imagine you are being interviewed by a top magazine or news outlet at your retirement. This interview will be read or viewed by your family, friends, children, grandchildren, and the world. This interview will cement your legacy and provide a marker in eternity of your impact on the human race. You sit down and are asked the questions below. Thoughtfully reflect on the interviewer's questions and journal your answers in the space below or in a notebook.

- What did I accomplish? What was my crowning accomplishment related to my purpose? What impact did my crowning achievement make?
- What achievements did I have along the way towards my crowning accomplishment?
- What gifts, talents, and strengths did I use to accomplish these things? What partnerships or collaborations did I have?
- Who did I serve along the way? How were they impacted by the accomplishments?
- Why did I accomplish what I did? What motivated and inspired my work?
- How did I accomplish it? What were some major steps or milestones along the way?
- Were there any 'big bets' or big risks that I took?
- When did these accomplishments, steps, and milestones occur?
- Where did I fail, and what did I learn? How did I grow from them?
- What was my ultimate takeaway to share with the world?

Interview Notes

_____

_____

_____

_____

_____

_____

_____

_____

_____

_____

Hopefully, you could imagine yourself in the future and clarify some of the major outcomes in your life that you would like to see come to fruition. I encourage you to sharpen the pencil on your life vision article. As a next step, take a look at your notes and actually try to write a professional news article on your life. I would encourage you to use a notebook and simply write about your life, beginning with the end in mind.

THE VISION STATEMENT

The article of your life is one major part of defining your vision. The exercise is meant to give you a full picture of your life, having accomplished your dreams in alignment with your purpose. However, a vision statement is a shortened version of your life vision boiled down to one or two sentences. It is similar to your purpose statement but focuses more on the actual accomplishment of a long-term goal. A vision statement is important because it is a simple reminder of the destination you have chosen for yourself. It is like a north star guiding you towards the achievement of the vision itself. The vision statement is succinct enough to drive the specific work focus while providing the energy of inspiration towards its achievement.

HOW TO WRITE A VISION STATEMENT

The vision statement is very simple in structure but can be challenging to write simply because it requires simplifying your life down into one or two (max) sentences. The basic construct consists of four elements:

- **To Be State** – The first part of the vision statement acknowledges that it will be manifested in the future. This can be captured with the words "To be" and "I will be."
- **The What** – The second part of the vision statement focuses on what you will become or what you want—the clearer, the better when it comes to defining your long-term vision.
- **Related to Your Why** – Your vision statement should be complimentary with your purpose. It is your purpose in pictures, the manifestation of your purpose in future outcomes.
- **Go Big** – Vision statements are big, bad, and bold. They represent the best of the best in a specific area or field. Go big or go home.

Example Vision Statements

Personal Vision Statements	Company Vision Statements
I will be a well-known leadership and personal development expert, improving millions of people's lives by expanding their knowledge, understanding, and application of purposeful leadership.	"To be the earth's most customer-centric company" ~ Amazon
To be a well-known and very capable engineer who solves challenging problems in the field of nuclear energy	"Striving to be the world's leader in patient experience, clinical outcomes, research and education" ~ Cleveland Clinic

To be the ultimate family man who took great care of my children and my children's children	"A world where everyone has a decent place to live" ~ Habitat for Humanity

VISION STATEMENT

Write down your vision statement below. What will you become that will reflect your greatness in your purpose?

_____

_____

_____

_____

_____

_____

_____

_____

_____

Now that you have your vision, you have a line of sight towards your best self. Now we must clarify what goals you must achieve in order to get to your vision and fully walk in your purpose.

STRATEGY AND GOALS

You now have your life purpose and the vision that you want for your life. The next focus is to break down your life's vision into manageable goals and create a strategy and plan to accomplish your life's vision. A strategy or a strategic plan is simply developing a set of steps towards a vision or goal. A strategy also informs us of what not to do. Strategy keeps us on track towards achieving a preferred end state. Strategies have been devised by military commanders and sports coaches to win the war or win the game. Businesses also have strategies. Business executives utilize strategy to determine the best use of their limited resources in order to beat the competition and win in the marketplace.

The strategy you will develop for yourself in order to attain your life's vision is exactly the same approach. You will determine how to best use your resources (strengths, talents, time, effort, and focus) towards the achievement of your vision. The best way to develop a strategy and plan towards achieving your vision is to break down the vision into interim goals.

Goals are what clarifies exactly what you want to achieve over time. Goals are key milestones along the way to your life vision that are set to achieve greatness. You can have clear goals without clarity of purpose or vision, but they become stronger when tied to them both.

Goals are also more effective if they are part of a strategy. In your case, the strategy will answer the question, "how will I best achieve my long-term vision?" A strategy is a plan of action. Inherent to strategy is choice. We are only allotted a certain amount of time and energy in a day, and we cannot do everything. You must choose how to spend your time, including what to say yes to and what to say no to. The combination of goals and strategy means that you must set goals to help you achieve the vision while considering which goals to go after first, second, third, etc. In other words, you must build a strategy that consists of prioritized goals and actions towards the achievement of your vision.

The steps in building the strategy are as follows:

1. Define Goals
2. Prioritize Goals
3. Determine Actions
4. Develop a Timeline

DEFINING GOALS

Goals are usually S.M.A.R.T. (i.e., specific, measurable, achievable, realistic, and time-based). Examples of S.M.A.R.T. goals include:

- I will be promoted from my current position to the next level within the next six months.
- I will write a book by the end of the year. ?
- I will research and choose my top 5 graduate school targets by September 1 that will catapult me in the field of cyber-security.?
- I will save six months of my salary within two years.

To help clarify your goals, ask yourself, "what are the top 20 goals I need to attain in my life in order to achieve my life's vision?" You will find that some goals will be short-term goals and achievable within the next 90 days. Other goals will be medium to long-term focused and may take five or ten years to accomplish. I'd suggest thinking about the top three to five goals that you would like to achieve in the following categories: business and career, health and wellness, family and relationships, and financial. Use the table below to list a few goals in each category. Feel free to use your own categories if there are things that you care about more deeply or are aligned to your purpose (e.g., Giving Back, Spiritual/Faith, etc.).

Remember to keep your purpose and life's vision top of mind as you fill in your goals. Your goals should help enable you to walk in your purpose and ultimately achieve your vision. Use a notebook or journal if you would like to write more extensively on your goals. Don't worry about the order of achieving the goals at this point. You will prioritize your goals and assign a clearer timeline to them in the next section.

Lastly, try to keep your goals simple and try not to overcomplicate them. I have provided additional worksheets in the appendix for all of these tables as well.

Business / Career	Health and Wellness	Family & Relationships	Financial

PRIORITIZING GOALS

If the world were a perfect place, we would have unlimited time to do everything we wanted at the same time. Unfortunately, the world doesn't work that way and we have to prioritize our time, energy, and focus. The prioritization of goals is the first step in determining how we will spend our time, manage our energy, and focus our efforts.

You can prioritize your goals by answering the following questions:

- Importance - Why is the goal important? What about this goal will allow you to achieve your life's vision and walk in your purpose?
- Timeline – When does this goal need to be accomplished to stay on track towards achieving my vision? Is this a near-term, medium-term, or long-term goal?
- Order – What sequence does this goal need to be accomplished in the context of other goals? What needs to, or should be, accomplished first, second, third, etc.?

List your set of goals for each of your categories in a separate table. Feel free to list these on a spreadsheet, Word table, or on journal pages. Additional worksheets are located in the appendix. You can also download copies on my website at www.anthonyperdue.com/purposetopower.

Business and Career			
Goal	Why Important?	Timeline	Order
Example: Get a promotion at work in my current field	I will have a greater impact on my customers, which will put me closer to my vision.	6 months	1

Once you have your goals put in the context of importance to your vision and purpose, along with timing and priority, you will create an overall plan of when each goal needs to be accomplished to achieve your vision. I would suggest you write down your ultimate vision or goal in each of the categories. The exercise of defining short, medium, and long-term goals should have helped you to clarify your top goal or ultimate destination in each category.

Begin the next exercise by prioritizing your ultimate vision for each category. These categorical visions should ultimately place you squarely in the midst of your ultimate life's vision. In other words, if you are able to accomplish the vision in each category, then you will have achieved your life's vision. You might find that one or more of your category visions aligned perfectly with your life's vision. If that's the case, that's okay. The next step will be most important in achieving that vision.

The next step is to list each of your goals in priority order that needs to be accomplished to arrive at your ultimate vision in that particular category. Worksheets are located in the appendix and on my website.

Business / Career	Health and Wellness	Family & Relationships	Financial
Example Vision: To become CEO of my own leadership company impacting at least 10,000 people annually.			

Example Goals:
1. Get a promotion within the next six months
2. Write a business plan within one year
3. Find investors for my business within 18 months

Once you have defined and prioritized your goals, write the action steps you need to take to achieve the goal. Use the table outline below to list your goals and action steps to achieve each goal. Remember to make your action items time-based by listing a date or the timeframe you expect to complete the action step. Try to be as exhaustive as possible with your action steps.

Business and Career

Your Top Three Goals	Action Items to Achieve Goals (list at least three)
Goal #1: Get a promotion with the next six months	1. Set up a meeting with my boss by the end of the week to let her know that I would like to be promoted within six months. 2. Develop a promotion plan with my boss within one month. 3. Ensure that I receive a great review by doing my best work daily.
Goal #2	
Goal #3	

I recognize that I am asking you to do quite a lot here. As Willie Jollie says, "you must get specific to be terrific!" Tony Robbins has a similar approach which he calls the "massive action plan." You must have a plan of action – a strategy – in order to achieve your vision, walk in your purpose, and unleash your power!

DR. ANTHONY PERDUE

CHAPTER 14

Execute!

"Only put off until tomorrow what you are willing to die having left undone."
——*Pablo Picasso*——

One of the most difficult challenges of most people is to execute their plans. You can have a clear purpose and vision and clear plans to get to your destination and still fail to get there. Trains have destinations with specific times of departure and arrival. Unfortunately, sometimes trains derail. Sometimes, something goes wrong, and the train comes off the track and fails to reach its destination.

Sometimes our lives can be much like the train. We can have great intentions and get derailed along the way towards our intended outcome.

There is an old saying, "the best-laid plans of mice and men often go awry." This is adapted from a line in the poem "To a Mouse" by Robert Burns. Most people don't know that Burns, a Scottish poet, wrote the poem while plowing in the field when he destroyed a mouse nest. The poor mouse never saw it coming. Even when we have our work cut out for us and begin executing, things can still go wrong, even to the point of giving up.

The famed boxer Iron Mike Tyson once famously said, "everyone has a plan until they get punched in the mouth." Life can sometimes punch us in the mouth, and plans go awry. For this reason, it is best to be proactive in managing the expected punches instead of just rolling with them. I assert that it is best to build up a good offense and a good defense in expectation of the punches coming your way.

There are three main efforts that you can put forth in order to prepare for life's punches in order to walk in your purpose and experience the power it has to offer:

1. Develop a Planning Habit
2. Manage Your Energy
3. Get Help and Accountability

DEVELOP THE HABIT OF PLANNING

As we have discovered, a well-laid strategy and plan is essential in walking in your purpose, advancing towards your vision and destiny, and ultimately experiencing your power. The challenge that we often face is that our plans can collect dust and not see the light of day. I used to be a business and IT strategy consultant for fortune 500 companies. One of the most memorable complaints from my customers was wasted money on strategy consultants. Can you imagine the pickle I often found myself in? I'm talking to a business prospect about engaging in a strategy development project, and they turn around to point to binders on the shelf that literally cost them more than a quarter-million dollars and were never used!
How did I overcome this dilemma, you might ask? I started strategy with *doing*. I would offer what we called a business value assessment that included both the strategy and planning work – and – the execution on a high-impact area of the business. In other words, I would offer that my team would walk and chew gum.
The worst thing you can do is to put your million-dollar plan on the shelf to collect dust. Your plan must not only get used, but be a part of your daily *doing*. There are many approaches to effective tactical plan-

ning. I've found that best practices revolve around establishing a routine or habit of planning around three main timeframes:

1. Quarterly – 30, 60, 90 days
2. Weekly
3. Daily

Quarterly Planning

A few years ago, I went to a telecom event where George Bush senior and Bill Clinton shared the stage. I point out that both men were there to protect you, yes you, against your mind running down a political rat hole in our polarized society. Look, while I do have my own personal political leanings, I'm willing to learn from anyone who has something of value to share. As George Bush spoke, he talked about a concept that he lived by called CAVU. He referenced CAVU as a phenomenon known as ceiling and visibility unlimited. He referred to CAVU as a mantra that he and his fellow World War II pilots would use in reference to their combat missions.

This mantra allowed him to think big and ultimately become the 41st President of the United States. I liken CAVU to your own vision and purpose. It is *your* unlimited ceiling and visibility that will allow you to accomplish great things in your life. While flying high for ultimate vision and visibility is necessary, sometimes we need to fly the plane at lower altitude levels to hit our target. While a long-term vision is necessary, short-term goals and action steps are necessary to hit our target. Quarterly planning is that lower altitude that allows us to get more tactical in our actions.

Quarterly planning has several advantages, including:

- Connects our long-term vision and goals to more tactical actions
- Allows for course correction and goals adjustment along the path to your vision

- Creates a manageable set of attainable tasks for action on a consistent basis
- Allows for the visualization of a "plan on a page" for you to stay focused
- It is motivating to see progress in smaller chunks that affect the big picture

The easiest way that I've found to plan quarterly is to create a 30-60-90 day plan. There are countless quarterly planner notebooks you can purchase or even software or apps that do that. You may even have your own approach to quarterly planning that has worked for you. Either way, I have created a quarterly planning template that you can use. The template has two distinct advantages: 1) It keeps the big picture, the CAVU in mind as it keeps your purpose, vision, and category vision front and center; 2) It provides the connection between your category vision and your 90-day goal, which allows you to connect your ultimate desired outcome to your short-term goals. Simply use the goals you seek to accomplish within the next 90 days from the goals and actions exercise that you completed in the previous chapter and add them to the quarterly planning worksheet.

Quarterly Planning Worksheet

My Purpose				
My Vision				
Category Vision	90 Day Goal	30 Day Plan	60 Day Plan	90 Day Plan

Weekly Planning

Weekly planning is simply the art of determining what you want to accomplish for that week. The simplest way I've found to plan your week is to a) determine which day will be the beginning of the week, b) determine what needs to get done for that week, and c) select which day(s) you will perform each action item that progresses you towards your goal.

Day to Begin the Week

Most of us have been trained to think of Monday as the beginning of our week. We have been indoctrinated to think this way because Monday is the day we usually begin working at our jobs, which is typically a day dedicated to the company that pays you a check. Monday is a good day to begin your week as it feels like a natural start of the week for most of us.

An alternative to starting your week on Monday is to start your week on Sunday instead. There are entire books written both historically and from a religious perspective on which days are considered the beginning and end of the week. Most have considered Sunday as the first day of the week and Saturday (the Sabbath) as the seventh day of the week, or what is also known as a day of rest, or historically a day of worship. Without going deep into the religious context, Sunday is actually the resurrection day or when the work begins.

If you start your work week on a Sunday, you can dedicate yourself to your purpose and vision, be it related to your corporate job or not, and have a clear calendar to schedule the action items and tasks that will get you closer to your goal. I prefer to look at Saturday as my day of rest, the day dedicated to my creator and family, and the day I dedicate to the restoration of my mind, soul, and body. The choice is yours as to which day is best, but it is a good practice to choose a consistent day.

Determine What Needs to Get Done That Week

One of the most satisfying rituals that I perform during weekly planning is the brain dump. I have a sheet of paper (or two) and simply write out everything that I need to do. My primary source of this list is from the Quarterly Planning Worksheet. I focus on the items that are prioritized in the 30-day planning window. I also jot down other pressing items that I need to get done that may be top of mind or from a list that I collect while on the go. I use a to-do app on my phone to capture action items at any given moment. World-renowned organization guru David Allen asserts getting the things to do out of your head and writing them down or listing them in an app can be a powerful productivity tool.

Days and Times for Tasks

Once you have a list of what needs to be done that week, you will determine which days will be dedicated to certain action items or tasks. The best practice is to plan this on the day before the start of your week. If you choose to start your week on a Sunday, then you would plan on Saturday. If you choose to start your week on a Monday, then Sunday would be the day (or evening) to plan your week.

Think about the priority items from your 30-day plan and your action item list, and determine which items are the most important to accomplish. Then create a bullet list for each day. Some action items or tasks may occupy multiple days, especially for daily habits that you are seeking to build daily (e.g., walking, journaling, or writing).

The last suggestion for weekly planning is to "calendarize" your items and schedule time to do your tasks as reflected on the planning template. If you use a digital calendar, you will find it easy to block time out for that specific task or set of listed tasks on each day.

Example Week Planning Template

Sunday	Monday	Tuesday	Wednesday	Thursday	Friday	Saturday

Daily Planning

One of my favorite personal development gurus is Brian Tracy. His lectures, books, and blogs on motivation, habit-forming, and planning are top-notch. I follow his advice for daily planning with his big three daily habits of successful people: 1) plan your day the night before, 2) set the priorities on your daily to-do list based upon the reality of the day, and 3) complete the most important task first.

Your weekly planning will show you what actions and activities you seek to accomplish by day, and if you calendarized, you will have the tasks also listed by time. Sometimes our lives can be dynamic, and things can change from day to day. I recommend that you follow Brian Tracy's advice and review your calendar the night before to ensure that nothing needs to be changed. Update your calendar to do the priority items first and schedule the most important task of the day the first thing in the morning.

With continual quarterly, weekly and daily planning, you will see your purpose and vision begin to come to fruition over time. If you would like to dive deeper on the subject of planning and organizing tasks, I would suggest reading, *The Seven Habits of Highly Successful People* by Stephen R. Covey and *Getting Things Done, The Art of Stress-Free Productivity* by David Allen. The better and more consistent you can get with your quarterly, weekly, and daily planning, particularly in the context of your purpose and vision, the more productive, energized, and powerful you will become!

MANAGE YOUR ENERGY

One of the biggest rituals that nearly everyone participates in is plugging in. We plug in our cell phones each and every day to recharge. We all look at our phones and either see the battery percentage sign or that little battery icon that indicates how much charge it has. All modern cell phones perform many tasks that contribute to our daily productivity, including talking, texting, browsing the web and social media, taking selfies, watching videos, using apps, and so on.

Human beings are the same way. We are productive daily with talking, typing, texting, reading, watching, working, walking, etc. We exert energy at every moment of the day. We are also just like a cell phone battery in that we need to recharge in order to be our most productive. In my experience as a leadership coach, I see a consistent theme with my clients: self-care and managing one's wellbeing are just as critical to leadership growth as improving leadership skills and competencies. In other words, to become your best self and become the best leader that you can be, you must proactively manage your ability to recharge yourself to 100% on a continual basis.

In their book, *The Power of Full Engagement*, Jim Loehr and Tony Schwartz assert that we must manage our energy and not our time. Like the battery of a cell phone, they suggest that we must recharge our batteries daily to be our most productive. They call the phenomenon of energy management "full engagement." It is our ability to be fully energized, fully present, and fully effective in our endeavors. The authors categorize our main sources of energy as: physical, mental, emotional, and spiritual. Being fully engaged allows us to feel confident, joyful, and connected. This is where we perform at our best and can pursue our purpose with our most energetic and invigorated selves.

Stephen R. Covey calls this same focused activity, sharpening the saw, and it is something that must be incorporated into our daily routine in order to stay sharp. Our saw must be sharp to keep chopping down trees (not the most environmentally friendly example I know).

Our energy and sharpness come from instituting daily habits that fill our spiritual, mental, emotional, and physical batteries. Dr. Johnny Parker calls these 'habits of greatness' or HOGS. These HOGS can be performed at any time, but most research suggests that sharpening the saw or managing your energy is best commenced in the morning. I suggest that you practice at least one activity in each of the four categories at least once per day, and preferably in the morning. These practices will help you manage and improve your energy for optimal performance.

The table below provides some high-level examples of daily practices you can use to manage your energy and improve your well-being. The appendix has more detail of best practices for you to adopt to manage your energy (see Well-Being Best Practices).

Spiritual	Mental	Emotional	Physical
Prayer	Learning	Gratitude	Sleep
Religious Study	Strengths Focus	Affirmations	Eat Properly
Meditation	Nature Walk	Self-Awareness	Exercise
Affirm Values	Planning	Journaling	Doctor / Dentist

BE HELD ACCOUNTABLE

There is an old scriptural saying that "Iron sharpens iron." The fact is, most of us operate more consistently and optimally when we are held in account by someone or something. You can most likely think of countless examples where accountability has driven you to perform your best, whether it was to prepare and study for a test, complete a work project, or train for a 5K. Being held accountable helps to produce results. Much like an athlete needs a coach or trainer, we can stand to gain from someone or a group of people who hold us accountable to our purpose, vision, and plans. Accountability can also keep us on track *when*, not if, you face headwinds and obstacles. No matter how much you progress towards a vision, goal, or destination, like Mike Tyson says, you will get "punched in the mouth." Life is just that way, whether you like it or not.

There are three effective means of being held accountable: sharing your plans with a friend or colleague, getting in a group of like-minded people, or using a coach. The first thing you can do is share your plans with someone you trust. A good friend or family member is a great place for accountability. In fact, when I coach leaders, the first question I ask after they commit to follow-up action is, "who can hold you accountable?" Accountability can make the difference between success and failure because your accountability partner can pick you up *when* you fall, and we *all* fall at some point.

The second means for accountability is through group accountability. This is where you communicate your plans to a group of like-minded people. One of the best forums I have seen for group accountability is forming small peer groups. These can be formed informally with people you trust and have the best interest of one another in mind and heart. These can also be more formalized through what's called a mastermind group. The mastermind group term was made famous in the early 20th century by Napoleon Hill and his world-renowned book *Think and Grow Rich*. Mastermind groups typically have a framework and approach to group accountability and can be extremely helpful in advancing your purpose, vision, and plans.

The last suggestion for accountability is to hire a life or leadership coach. In the 2016 NBA Eastern Conference Finals between the Cleveland Cavaliers and the Toronto Raptors, the Raptors were pronounced dead on arrival by reporters and pundits alike. Cleveland took a 2 – 0 lead in the best of three series. Keep in mind; this was the LeBron James' led Cleveland Cavaliers. While down two games, Toronto head coach Dwane Casey reminded his team, "Let's go out and play with pride," stating, "We can't just be satisfied to be here. My goal for this organization, this franchise, is to win a championship." Toronto would go on to win the next two games and tie the series 2 – 2. Although they would eventually fall in game five, the lesson here is that the coach helped

Toronto believe in themselves and fight back against a world champion in LeBron James.

While leadership coaches are not leaders of sports teams, they can be effective with their clients and improve their outcomes through motivation, accountability, and overcoming obstacles. In fact, a great coach can help you through the process of finding and clarifying your purpose, vision, and roadmap.

Whichever means of accountability you choose, I encourage you to invest the time and effort into finding it. Accountability can be the difference between a purpose, vision, and plan on the shelf collecting dust, and consistent execution over time on a road less traveled, but each day getting you closer to your destiny.

CHAPTER 15

Purpose to Power: The Conclusion

"Everyone has a purpose in life and a unique talent to give to others. And when we blend this unique talent with service to others, we experience the ecstasy and exultation of our own spirit, which is the ultimate goal of all goals."
—*Kallam Anji Reddy*—

I'd like you to take a moment and close your eyes. Wait, don't close your eyes yet! Read this paragraph first! Think about the reason that you've read this book. Imagine yourself five or ten years from now, putting all of these thoughts and frameworks into practice. Try to visualize yourself in the state of walking in your purpose, being an embodiment of your purpose in pictures, confidently walking and working your plan, and being the best [insert your name here] that you can be. Think about your life's different areas and what becoming the best version of yourself in those various areas looks like. Close your eyes and take two or three minutes to see the new you.

Cheater! I knew you couldn't close your eyes! I'm just kidding, of course. I know it is difficult to do, but visualization can be a very powerful technique to give yourself a glimpse into your future self. I believe that you've gotten this far in the book because of who you want to become and not for who you have been already. It is the burden you have inside to become your best self and to self-actualize. In other words, you desire to manifest yourself into your best self, and I KNOW that you can do it!

THE NEW WORLD

For some of you, purpose may be a new discovery, and for you, I applaud you. It will feel like a newly minted yacht, leaving a dock towards your destiny. For others, you may already be walking in your purpose, but perhaps you didn't know it, or you've now got more clarity – perhaps high-definition clarity. If this is you, you are now able to set your course with more confidence and strength and continue down the road on the journey with greater conviction, effort, energy, and effectiveness, with the ability to produce ten times as much of what you produced before! In either situation, you are now in a position where you can harness your power. Your purpose is your power!

EXPERIENCING PURPOSE TO POWER

So how will you know if you are experiencing purpose to power? I offer four main elements that you will experience in your life to a greater degree, which will provide you with evidence. The first element is known as *flow*. Flow is a state of being when you are in such a zone that you feel like you are putting forth little to no effort in your work. It is a feeling much like being in a tunnel blocked out from the rest of the world only focused on what you love and that you feel very passionate about. I've had the wonderful experience of feeling this flow while writing this book. I could actually visualize myself talking to, and coaching, great individuals and leaders such as yourself. In flow, social media can also almost become non-existent. Checking email inboxes becomes something you'll get to eventually, because its importance pails in comparison to your purposeful actions. Flow will make you feel as though you are flying in the moment like an eagle while doing your life's work and being your best self.

The second element of experiencing purpose to power is the clarity and understanding of the value that you give to the world. You will know your infinite value to your customers, colleagues, family, friends, or business associates. That value is massive, and you know it! You will know without a shadow of a doubt that your best work translates into enormous value to those who are the recipients of your purposeful work and purposeful energy. You will be keenly aware that your core values are core values to others. Whether it is your ability to create written content, art, music, or business plans, your value is golden. Perhaps your value is your keen awareness of people and your ability to empathize with others, which puts you in a great position to solve their biggest problems. Or perhaps you are so detail-oriented that you can help others get and stay organized or interpret data or numbers like no other. Your skills, competencies, and strengths are verifiable by others, and you get complimented on the work you do. Whatever your values, competencies, gifts, talents, and strengths are, they show up, and they give you and the world – *power*!

The third element of experiencing purpose to power is greater *energy*. Have you ever seen the Red Bull commercial that says, "it gives you wings?" Well, that's the feeling you get when you are walking in your purpose. You have so much energy that you believe you can fly! You might not literally be able to fly, but the energy you gain from walking in your purpose feels like a literal power source. You don't need the caffeine and stimulants of Red Bull because your purpose gives you that stimulation. The study of positive psychology reveals that there are actually scientific reasons for that energy. It is one reason you should do your purposeful work in the morning because it actually makes you feel better. Now that's not to say that you will never feel tired or need restoration after giving of yourself, but in that moment, those endorphins and chemicals will actually make you feel as though you've got wings.

The last element of experiencing purpose to power is that you will work tactically but think strategically. In other words, you can focus on the work that matters to the long-term vision. In Japanese culture, this is known as Hoshin Kanri. With Hoshin Kanri, you never do short-term work that sacrifices the long-term vision. This also allows you to know that *not* to do.

As I mentioned in a previous chapter, we are constantly bombarded by what the world wants from us. The majority of what it wants is your time, focus, and energy. Your time, energy, and focus equal money, albeit for someone else. Time spent on social media, time spent on websites, time spent shopping on Amazon, and even time spent on requests from friends, family, and colleagues all represent time wanted from you for their benefit (usually financial). You will know what is not core to your purpose, vision, and values. You will have the knowledge to know how to better spend your precious time, focus, and energy, along with the knowledge of what activities *not* to engage in.

One quick note I wish to interject here on choosing what not to do. In the book, *The 4-Hour Workweek*, Tim Ferriss discusses knowing what to do versus what to outsource. This concept was hit home hard by Tim and tends to be a boon for how many entrepreneurs do business. You should know what is *not* core to your values and strengths and find people who do it better.

These four indicators will give you insight and knowledge that you are walking, working, and living in your purpose. The endorphins and chemicals emitted from your brain from being in a state of flow, from leveraging your values and strengths, from the energy you will receive, and thinking and acting strategically will make you feel like you've got wings.

I've written this book for those who want to be their best selves and experience a life of purpose and power. You should not only know your purpose but possess a roadmap for life to achieve your dreams, goals, and vision.

I'll leave you with two quotes from the great motivational speaker Zig Ziglar. "You can get everything in life *you want* if you help enough other people get what *they want*." I believe that Mr. Ziglar knew that service to others, *in your purpose*, with the best of who you are gives you a ticket to your dreams and even financial benefits.

The second thing that Zig Ziglar used to say is that "I will see you at the top." My friend, I know that you will make it to the top if you follow your purpose, develop your purpose in pictures, plan your road, and begin to execute your journey. Your power awaits, and I pray that you will experience it to the fullest.

Appendix

STORY OUTLINE

Time Frame	Introduction	Rising Moment / Climax	Falling Action / Conclusion	Theme / Moral of the Story

- Acceptance
- Achievement
- Advancement
- Promotion
- Adventure
- Affection
- Altruism
- Arts
- Awareness
- Beauty
- Challenge
- Change
- Community
- Compassion
- Competence
- Competition
- Completion
- Connectedness
- Cooperation
- Collaboration
- Country
- Creativity
- Decisiveness
- Democracy
- Design
- Discovery
- Diversity
- Environmental
- Excellence Excitement
- Experiment
- Expertise
- Awareness
- Economic Security
- Education
- Effectiveness
- Efficiency
- Elegance
- Entertainment
- Enlightenment
- Equality
- Ethics
- Fairness
- Fame
- Family
- Fast Pace
- Freedom
- Friendship
- Fun
- Grace
- Growth
- Happiness
- Harmony
- Health
- Helping Others
- Helping Society
- Honesty
- Humor
- Imagination
- Improvement
- Independence
- Influencing
- Inner Harmony
- Inspiration
- Integrity
- Ministering
- Money
- Morality
- Mystery
- Intellect
- Involvement
- Knowledge
- Leadership
- Learning
- Loyalty
- Magnificence
- Making a Difference
- Mastery
- Meaningful Work
- Openness
- Order
- Passion
- Peace
- Personal Development
- Personal Expression
- Planning
- Play
- Pleasure
- Power
- Privacy
- Purity
- Quality
- Radiance
- Recognition
- Relationships
- Religion
- Reputation
- Responsibility
- Unity
- Variety
- Wealth
- Winning
- Accountability
- Risk
- Safety
- Security
- Self-Respect
- Sensibility
- Sensuality
- Serenity
- Service
- Sexuality
- Sophistication
- Spark
- Speculation
- Spirituality
- Stability
- Status
- Success
- Teaching
- Tenderness
- Thrill

VISION STATEMENT

Write your vision statement below. What will you become that will reflect your greatness in your purpose?

_____

_____

_____

_____

_____

_____

_____

_____

_____

_____

_____

_____

GOALS WORKSHEET

Business / Career	Health and Wellness	Family & Relationships	Financial

GOAL PRIORITIZATION WORKSHEETS

Category:

Goal	Why Important?	Timeline	Order

Category:

Goal	Why Important?	Timeline	Order

Category:

Goal	Why Important?	Timeline	Order

ACTION PLANS TO ACHIEVE GOALS

CATEGORY:

Goals List	Action Items to Achieve Goals (list at least three)
Goal #1	
Goal #2	
Goal #3	
Goal #4	
Goal #5	
Goal #6	

CATEGORY:

Goals List	Action Items to Achieve Goals (list at least three)
Goal #1	
Goal #2	
Goal #3	
Goal #4	
Goal #5	
Goal #6	

CATEGORY:

Goals List	Action Items to Achieve Goals (list at least three)
Goal #1	
Goal #2	
Goal #3	
Goal #4	
Goal #5	
Goal #6	

WELL-BEING BEST PRACTICES

Spiritual

- **Strengthen Belief System** - Engage more in prayer and/or study of your belief system.
- **Clarify Your Values** - Be clear of your top three to five values and seek to include living your values (aka character) daily.
- **Clarify Your Purpose** - Your purpose is your big WHY, mission, the reason for being, and the reason for your life and/or work. The clearer you are about your purpose and align it to your work and daily actions, the more energy derived from your activities.
- **Meditate** - Meditation and breathing exercises can be a way to connect spiritually.

Emotional

- **Gratitude Journal** - Gratitude journal is one of the best ways to lift your spirits and promote wellbeing. Write at least five things that you are grateful for and why daily.
- **Increase Emotional Awareness** - Journal your emotions (what were you feeling). Also, journal what triggered your emotions, paying special attention to negative emotions (anger, anxiety, worry, etc.). Write down your responses to negative emotions and the outcomes. Write down what you could have done differently to react and plan how you will react the next time you start feeling those emotions.

Mental

- **Strengths Focus** - Focus on your strengths and begin your day by engaging in your strengths. Strengths come in two flavors, competencies and character (values in action). Can improve self-regard and self-actualization.

- **Clarify Vision** - Clarify your future vision and goals. Your vision is your purpose in pictures and helps with self-actualization (becoming your best self).
- **Limit Screen Time** - Social media and phone usage can become addictive and cause us to lose focus (social media companies use the same techniques as the gambling industry to activate the very same brain mechanisms that are triggered from the use of cocaine in order to get you to engage on their platforms in order to maximize their profits!).
- **Develop Rituals** - Developing rituals (particularly in the morning and evening) has many benefits. Most billionaires have morning rituals where they are extremely productive prior to 8 am!
- **Practice Self-development** - Learning is lifelong. Learners are earners! Continue to take classes, read non-fiction, spend time with smart people that pour into you.
- **Plan Your Day** - Planning your day is an effective means to reduce anxiety and worry, making you more productive.

Physical

- **Eat Properly** - Eat lower glycemic index foods (foods with less sugar). Eat more whole foods (vegetables and fruits). Watch your calories and eat less. Exercise more.
- **Get 8 Hours of Sleep** - Studies show that getting 8 hours of sleep is good for restoration and energy. Get an eye mask to help block out light and create more melatonin.
- **Exercise** - Exercise is great for energy and can help boost our moods.
- **Schedule Doctor and Dentist Appointments** - Keep up with your physical health by getting checkups.

References

Chapter 1

Staff, C. D. T. (2021, June 24). *Ask a scientist: How many solar systems are in the universe?* Columbia Daily Tribune. https://eu.columbiatribune.com/

Redd, N. T. (2019, February 7). *How Old Is Earth?* Space.Com. https://www.space.com/24854-how-old-is-earth.html

Masters, K. (2021). *How many known galaxies are there? (Intermediate).* Curious About Astronomy? Ask an Astronomer. http://curious.astro.cornell.edu/about-us/95-the-universe/galaxies/general-questions/516-how-many-known-galaxies-are-there-intermediate

Redd, N. T. (2018, March 7). *How Fast Does Light Travel? | The Speed of Light.* Space.Com. https://www.space.com/15830-light-speed.html

Earth Compared to the Universe. (2014, July 4). Futurism. https://futurism.com/earth-compared-to-the-universe

Redd, N. T. (2017b, June 7). *How Big is the Universe?* Space.Com. https://www.space.com/24073-how-big-is-the-universe.html

Egg meets sperm (article) | Embryology. (2021). Khan Academy. https://www.khanacademy.org/test-prep/mcat/cells/embryology/a/egg-meets-sperm

Mother To Son By Langston Hughes, Famous Family Poem. (2016). Family Friend Poems. https://www.familyfriendpoems.com/poem/mother-to-son-by-langston-hughes

Good Therapy Editor Team. (2019). *Self-Actualization.* Www.Goodtherapy.Org. https://www.goodtherapy.org/learn-about-therapy/issues/self-actualization

Karahanna, E., Xu, S. X., & Zhang, N. (. (2015). *Psychological Ownership Motivation and Use of Social Media.* Journal of Marketing Theory and Practice, 23(2), 185-207.

Abel, J. I., Buff, C. L., & O'Neill, J.,C. (2013). *Actual self-concept versus ideal self-concept.* Sport, Business and Management, 3(1), 78-96.

Busby, M. (2018, May 8). *Social media copies gambling methods "to create psychological cravings."* The Guardian. https://www.theguardian.com/technology/2018/may/08/social-media-copies-gambling-methods-to-create-psychological-cravings

(2021, February 4). *Dopamine, Smartphones & You: A battle for your time.* Science in the News. https://sitn.hms.harvard.edu/flash/2018/dopamine-smartphones-battle-time/

Gates, H. L. (2017, January 12). *How Many Slaves Landed in the US?* The Root. https://www.theroot.com/how-many-slaves-landed-in-the-us-1790873989

Gaskin, Darrell J., Alvin E. Headen, and Shelley White-means. *Racial Disparities in Health and Wealth: The Effects of Slavery and Past Discrimination.* Review of Black Political Economy 32, no. 3-4 (Winter, 2005): 95-110.

Allan, P. O., & Harrington, R. (2002). *The relationships among black consciousness, self-esteem, and academic self-efficacy in african american men.* The Journal of Psychology, 136(2), 214-24.

Mason, P. L. (2017). *Not black-alone: The 2008 presidential election and racial self-identification among african americans.* Review of Black Political Economy, 44(1-2), 55-76.

Chapter 2

Definition of purpose | Dictionary.com. (2002). Www.Dictionary.Com. https://www.dictionary.com/browse/purpose

(2021b, February 5). *Rick Warren to Speak at Proclaim 19 Convention in Anaheim –.* NRB. https://nrb.org/articles/rick-warren-to-speak-at-proclaim-19-convention-in-anaheim/

Strong's Greek: 1014. βούλομαι (boulomai) -- to will. (2004). Bible Hub. https://biblehub.com/greek/1014.htm

Salisbury, S. (2019, October 21). *Take a cue from Martin Luther King Jr. on how powerful purpose transforms.* Biz Journals. https://www.bizjournals.com/chicago/news/2019/10/21/mlk-jr-shows-how-powerful-purpose-transforms.html

"I've Been to the Mountaintop" by Dr. Martin Luther King, Jr. (2021). AFSCME. https://www.afscme.org/about/history/mlk/mountaintop

Witherington (2011). *Work - A Kingdom Perspective on Labor*

Dhingra, M., & Dhingra, V. (2011). *Perception Scriptures' Perspective.* Journal of Human Values, 17(1), 63-72.

Maisel Ph.D., E. (2012, November 16). *Why Choosing Your Life Purpose Is So Darn Hard.* Https://Www.Psychologytoday.Com/Us/Blog/Rethinking-Mental-Health/201211/Why-Choosing-Your-Life-Purpose-Is-so-Darn-Hard. https://www.psychologytoday.com/us/blog/rethinking-mental-health/201211/why-choosing-your-life-purpose-is-so-darn-hard

Hultman, K., Gellermann, B., Beckhard, R., & Adams, J. D. (2001). *Balancing Individual and Organizational Values.* Wiley.

Loehr, J. (2005). *The Power of Full Engagement: Managing Energy, Not Time, Is the Key to High Performance and Personal (Reprint).* FreePress.

Drageset, Jorunn & Haugan, Gørill & Tranvåg, Oscar. (2017). *Crucial aspects promoting meaning and purpose in life: Perceptions of nursing home residents.* BMC Geriatrics. 17. 10.1186/s12877-017-0650-x.

Swaniker, F. (2018, May 27). *Resist that calling. It's probably not your purpose in life.* Medium. https://medium.com/@FredSwaniker/resist-that-calling-it-s-probably-not-your-purpose-in-life-1dd33a297185

Rifkind, Hugo. *The Meaning of Life in Four Pages: How to be Smarter Get Up to Speed on 24 Centuries of Thought, the History of Britain and the Best Bits of Shakespeare in our Instant Wisdom Series.* Day 1: The 15-Minute Philosophy Guide (from Plato to Sartre)." The Times, Sep 22, 2012.

ReShel, A. (2021, May 3). *Platos Approach to Life.* UPLIFT. https://uplift.love/platos-approach-to-life/

(2014, October 11). *Aristotle's Purpose of Life*. The Great Conversation. https://orwell1627.wordpress.com/2013/06/30/aristotles-purpose-of-life/

Lewis, J. S., & Geroy, G. D. (2000). *Employee spirituality in the workplace: A cross-cultural view for the management of spiritual employees.* Journal of Management Education, 24(5), 682-694.

Hultman, K., Gellermann, B., Beckhard, R., & Adams, J. D. (2001). *Balancing Individual and Organizational Values*. Wiley.

Kashdan Ph.D., T. (2015, February 24). *What Do Scientists Know About Finding a Purpose in Life?* Psychology Today. https://www.psychologytoday.com/us/blog/curious/201502/what-do-scientists-know-about-finding-purpose-in-life

Chapter 3

Oxford University Press (OUP). (2021). *power*. Lexico.Com. https://www.lexico.com/en/definition/power

Klein, S. (2017, December 7). *100 Wonderful Ways To Live To 100*. HuffPost. https://www.huffpost.com/entry/100-ways-live-to-100_n_3956896

Panel, O. M. S. W. I., & Committee, O. N. S. (2013). *Subjective Well-Being: Measuring Happiness, Suffering, and Other Dimensions of Experience.* Washington, D.C., US: National Academies Press. Retrieved from http://0-www.ebrary.com.library.regent.edu

Michaelson, J., Mahony, S. & Schifferes, J. (2012). *Measuring Well-being A guide for practitioners. new economics foundation.* Retrieved from http://www2.warwick.ac.uk/fac/med/research/platform/wemwbs/researchers/userguide/nef_measuring-well-being-handbook-final.pdf

European Social Survey (2013). *Measuring and Reporting on Europeans' Wellbeing, Findings from the European Social Survey.* Retrieved from http://www.europeansocialsurvey.org/docs/findings/ESS1-6_measuring_and_reporting_on_europeans_wellbeing.pdf

Huppert, F., Marks, N., Michaelson, J., Vázquez, C., Vitterso., J. (2013). *Personal and social well-being: Round 6 Personal and Social Wellbeing* - Final Module in Template. European Social Survey. Retrieved from http://www.europeansocialsurvey.org/docs/round6/questionnaire/ESS6_final_personal_and_social_well_being_module_template.pdf

Harvard Health. (2019, November 28). *Will a purpose-driven life help you live longer?* https://www.health.harvard.edu/blog/will-a-purpose-driven-life-help-you-live-longer-2019112818378

Perry, S. (2019, June 11). *Having a life purpose linked to longer life, study finds.* MinnPost. https://www.minnpost.com/second-opinion/2019/06/having-a-life-purpose-linked-to-longer-life-study-finds/

Tv, C. (2017, November 1). *Jim Rohn On Purpose, Self Confidence, Enthusiasm, Expertise and Preparation.* YouTube. https://www.youtube.com/watch?v=I1o0_L40kOc&feature=youtu.be

Loehr, J., & Schwartz, T. (2021). *The Power of Full Engagement: Managing Energy, Not Time, Is the Key to High Performance and Personal Renewal.* Free Press.

Ramakrishna Rao, K. *Mahatma Gandhi's Pragmatic Spirituality: Its Relevance to Psychology East and West.* Psychol Stud 63, 109–116 (2018). https://doi.org/10.1007/s12646-017-0394-x

History.com Editors. (2020, September 15). *Gandhi begins fast in protest of caste separation.* HISTORY. https://www.history.com/this-day-in-history/gandhi-begins-fast-in-protest-of-caste-separation

How Many iPhones Have Been Sold Worldwide? (2019, December 27). Lifewire. https://www.lifewire.com/how-many-iphones-have-been-sold-1999500

Linkedin. (2016). *2016 Global Report: Purpose at Work.* https://business.linkedin.com/content/dam/me/business/en-us/talent-solutions/resources/pdfs/purpose-at-work-global-report.pdf

TAP - MHS Assessments. (2021). Multi-Health Systems. https://tap.mhs.com/Account/Login.aspx?ReturnUrl=%2fEQi20Manual%2fpart1%2fEqiFramework.html

Chapter 5

Monarth, H. (2015, December 10). *The Irresistible Power of Storytelling as a Strategic Business Tool*. Harvard Business Review. https://hbr.org/2014/03/the-irresistible-power-of-storytelling-as-a-strategic-business-tool

Newton, P. (2009, April 26). *What Is Dopamine? The neurotransmitter's role in the brain and behavior*. Psychology Today. https://www.psychologytoday.com/us/blog/mouse-man/200904/what-is-dopamine

King, H. M. (2005). *How Do Diamonds Form? | They Don't Form From Coal!* Geology.Com. https://geology.com/articles/diamonds-from-coal/

Bunting, J. (2021, April 3). *Freytag's Pyramid: Definition, Examples, and How to Use this Dramatic Structure in Your Writing*. The Write Practice. https://thewritepractice.com/freytags-pyramid/

Chapter 6

Bertolini, S. (2018, September 30). *« Know thyself »*. Ancient Greek Courses. https://ancientgreekcourses.com/anthropology/know-thyself/

Leary, M. R., & Tangney, J. P. (Eds.). (2003). *Handbook of self and identity*. The Guilford Press.

Morin, A. (2006). *Levels of consciousness and self-awareness: A comparison and integration of various neurocognitive views. Consciousness and Cognition*, 15(2), 358-371. doi:10.1016/j.concog.2005.09.006

Perdue, A. (Host). (2019, September). Patt Steiner. Discussion on Self-Awareness.

Ashley, G. C., & Reiter-Palmon, R. (2012). *Self-awareness and the evolution of leaders: The need for a better measure of self-awareness*. Journal of Behavioral and Applied Management, 14(1), 2-17.

Trapnell, P. D., & Campbell, J. D. (1999). *Private self-consciousness and the five-factor model of personality: Distinguishing rumination from reflection*. Journal of Personality and Social Psychology, 76(2), 284–304. https://doi.org/10.1037/0022-3514.76.2.284

Manson, M. (2016). *The subtle art of not giving a xxxx: A counterintuitive approach to living a good life*.

Burton, N. (2015, August 28). *The Psychology of Self-Deception A short, sharp look into some of our most important ego defenses.* Psychology Today. https://www.psychologytoday.com/us/blog/hide-and-seek/201508/the-psychology-self-deception

Self-Deception (Stanford Encyclopedia of Philosophy). (2016, November 7). Plato Institute. https://plato.stanford.edu/entries/self-deception/

Chapter 7

Hultman, K., & Gellermann, W. (2002). *Balancing individual and organizational values : walking the tightrope to success / Ken Hultman, with Bill Gellermann ; with forewords by Richard Beckhard and John D. Adams.* San Francisco, CA : Jossey-Bass/Pfeiffer, c2002.

Burton, N. (2012, May 23). *Our Hierarchy of Needs True freedom is a luxury of the mind. Find out why.* Psychology Today. https://www.psychologytoday.com/us/blog/hide-and-seek/201205/our-hierarchy-needs

Loehr, J., & Schwartz, T. (2021). *The Power of Full Engagement: Managing Energy, Not Time, Is the Key to High Performance and Personal Renewal.* Free Press.

Jung, C. G. (1958). *The undiscovered self.* New York: New American Library.

Chapter 8

Kerfoot, K. (2005). *Signature strengths: Achieving your destiny.* Nursing Economics, 23(1), 46-8. Retrieved from https://search-proquest-com.proxydc.wrlc.org/docview/236935712?accountid=28903

Drucker, P. F. (1999). *Managing Oneself. Harvard Business Review,* 77(2), 64. https://link.gale.com/apps/doc/A54077791/AONE?u=anon~3d43a1d7&sid=googleScholar&xid=51fdd2d2

Jackson, N. F. (2003). *Now, discover your strengths: How to develop your talents and those of people you manage:* EMJ. Engineering Management Journal, 15(1), 34-35. Retrieved from https://search-proquest-com.proxydc.wrlc.org/docview/208995903?accountid=28903

Hultman, K., & Gellermann, W. (2002). *Balancing individual and organizational values : walking the tightrope to success / Ken Hultman, with Bill Gellermann ; with forewords by Richard Beckhard and John D. Adams*. San Francisco, CA : Jossey-Bass/Pfeiffer, c2002.\

Harzer, C., & Ruch, W. (2016). Your strengths are calling: Preliminary results of a web-based strengths intervention to increase calling. Journal of Happiness Studies, 17(6), 2237-2256. doi:http://dx.doi.org.proxydc.wrlc.org/10.1007/s10902-015-9692-y

Rath, T., & Conchie, B. (2008). *Strengths Based Leadership: Great Leaders, Teams, and Why People Follow* (1st ed.). Gallup Press.

Zenger, J., & Folkman, J. (2019). *The New Extraordinary Leader, 3rd Edition: Turning Good Managers into Great Leaders* (3rd ed.). McGraw-Hill Education.

Chapter 9

TAP - MHS Assessments. (2021b). Multi Health Systems. https://tap.mhs.com/Account/Login.aspx?ReturnUrl=%2fmanuals%2feqi20manual%2fpart1%2fEqiFramework.html

History.com Editors. (2021, April 30). *MADD founder's daughter killed by drunk driver*. HISTORY. https://www.history.com/this-day-in-history/madd-founders-daughter-killed-by-drunk-driver

Connley, C. (2018, May 8). *Richard Branson on the key lesson about fear he learned from Dr. Dre and Jimmy Iovine*. CNBC. https://www.cnbc.com/2018/05/08/what-richard-branson-learned-about-fear-from-dr-dre-and-jimmy-iovine.html

(2018, June 1). *Interscope Records Founder Jimmy Iovine Reveals the 1 Thing That Made Him a Success*. Complex. https://www.complex.com/music/2017/07/jimmy-iovine-reveals-the-1-thing-that-made-him-a-success

Thomas, E. (2016, April 1). *What Causes Fear?* Effective Mind Control. https://www.effective-mind-control.com/what-causes-fear.html

Chapter 10

National Geographic Society. (2012, October 9). *compass*. https://www.nationalgeographic.org/encyclopedia/compass/

Jessa, T. (2015, December 24). *How Does a Compass Work*. Universe Today. https://www.universetoday.com/77072/how-does-a-compass-work/

Covey, S. (2021). *First Things First by Stephen R. Covey (20-Jan-2003) Paperback*. Pocket Books; Export ed edition (20 Jan. 2003).

Chapter 11

Taylor, C. (2020, June 19). *The Underrated Way for Career Changers to Get Experience in Their New Field*. The Muse. https://www.themuse.com/advice/the-underrated-way-for-career-changers-to-get-experience-in-their-new-field

Lavender, C. (2014, Oct 11). Recent cancer survivor finds purpose in volunteering. *TCA Regional News*

Essick, K. (2014, Jun 23). Encore (A special report) --- second acts: Her mission: Every woman works. *Wall Street Journal*

Hill, N., & Horowitz, M. (2019). *Think and Grow Rich (Original Classic Edition)* (Original ed.). G&D Media.

Chapter 13

The Henry Ford. (2021). *Thomas Edison - Visionaries on Innovation*. https://www.thehenryford.org/explore/stories-of-innovation/visionaries/thomas-edison

ABOUT THE AUTHOR

Dr. Anthony M. Perdue is a leadership development coach and trainer. He has over 25 years of experience working with executives from companies such as Lyft, Verizon, IBM, and General Motors. Anthony has a passion for helping people develop and walk in their purpose, focusing on developing purposeful leaders. He provides leadership training and coaching covering topics including purposeful leadership, self-awareness, self-care and well-being, emotional intelligence, core ideology, positive psychology, and strategic leadership.

Dr. Perdue is also an adjunct professor of leadership and teaches systems and organizational leadership to PhD and Graduate students. He is a certified emotional intelligence trainer and coach, and has certifications in both professional and business coaching. He is a graduate of Regent University with a Doctor of Strategic Leadership (DSL) and Duke University, the Fuqua School of Business, with a Master of Business Administration.

www.ingramcontent.com/pod-product-compliance
Lightning Source LLC
Chambersburg PA
CBHW071832080526
44589CB00012B/998